Lecture Notes in Computer Science 11455

Commenced Publication in 1973
Founding and Former Series Editors:
Gerhard Goos, Juris Hartmanis, and Jan van Leeuwen

More information about this series at http://www.springer.com/series/7412

Bertrand Kerautret · Miguel Colom ·
Daniel Lopresti · Pascal Monasse ·
Hugues Talbot (Eds.)

Reproducible Research in Pattern Recognition

Second International Workshop, RRPR 2018
Beijing, China, August 20, 2018
Revised Selected Papers

 Springer

Editors
Bertrand Kerautret
LIRIS
Université de Lyon 2
Bron, France

Daniel Lopresti
Department of Computer Science
and Engineering
Lehigh University
Bethlehem, PA, USA

Hugues Talbot
CentraleSupelec
Universite Paris-Saclay
Gif-sur-Yvette, France

Miguel Colom
CMLA, ENS Cachan, CNRS
Université Paris-Saclay
Cachan, France

Pascal Monasse
Laboratoire d'Informatique Gaspard-Monge
Ecole des Ponts Paristech
Marne-la-Vallée, France

ISSN 0302-9743   ISSN 1611-3349 (electronic)
Lecture Notes in Computer Science
ISBN 978-3-030-23986-2   ISBN 978-3-030-23987-9 (eBook)
https://doi.org/10.1007/978-3-030-23987-9

LNCS Sublibrary: SL6 – Image Processing, Computer Vision, Pattern Recognition, and Graphics

This Springer imprint is published by the registered company Springer Nature Switzerland AG
The registered company address is: Gewerbestrasse 11, 6330 Cham, Switzerland

Preface

This volume contains the articles from the second edition of the Workshop on Reproducible Research in Pattern Recognition that was held during August 20, 2018, in conjunction with ICPR 2018 in Beijing. It followed in the same spirit as the first edition with a special focus on digital geometry and mathematical morphology. It was intended as both a short participative course on reproducible research (RR) aspects leading to open discussions with the participants and also on how to actually perform RR. For this second edition, a new call for short papers was proposed to the ICPR authors. The main idea was to give authors of already accepted ICPR papers the possibility to highlight the reproducibility of their work with a companion paper. It was an opportunity to include implementation details, source code descriptions, parameter choice etc.

This proceedings volume gathers 14 contributions covering the RR result track (three papers), invited RR contributions (five papers), and the new companion paper tracks (six papers). The contributions were reviewed by an average of 2.35 reviewers and the short papers were generally given two assessments: one for the short paper itself and another from the RR label linked to the code repository (when authors apply for the label). A comparable number of participants were present in this workshop with around 25 participants. The public participated actively in the discussions with presenters focusing on RR. The number of authors increased by over 45% for this second edition with 41 different authors.

From all the contributions, two invited talks opened the workshop. The first was related to the evolution and the future of the *IPOL* journal, including a new structure for machine learning applications. The second invited talk focused on a review of reproducible research platforms with an overview of the most recents means of publication. The three main papers on RR results were oral presentations and four short papers were oral fast-track presentations. In addition to these new classic presentations, a new type of practical session was proposed by Miguel Colom with "Hands on IPOL Demonstration System" where users were able to construct their own online demonstration from a simple description file.

As in the first edition, the RRPR workshop received the endorsement of the International Association of Pattern Recognition (IAPR). We would like to thank this association as well as all authors who contributed to these proceedings. We also thank the Springer computer sciences team and in particular Alfred Hofman and Anna Kramer, for allowing to us once again to publish the proceedings as an LNCS volume. Finally, we also thank Jean-Michel Morel for supporting our initiative and Audrey Bichet of the MMI department of Saint Dié-des-Vosges for designing a new poster for this workshop.

March 2019

Bertrand Kerautret
Miguel Colom
Daniel Lopresti
Pascal Monasse
Hugues Talbot

Organization

Chairs

Bertrand Kerautret   LIRIS, Université de Lyon 2, France
Miguel Colom   CMLA, ENS Paris Saclay, France
Bart Lamiroy   LORIA, Université de Lorraine, France
Daniel Lopresti   CSE, Lehigh University, USA
Pascal Monasse   LIGM, École des Ponts, France
Jean-Michel Morel   CMLA, ENS Paris Saclay, France
Fabien Pierre   LORIA, Université de Lorraine, France
Hugues Talbot   CentraleSupelec, Universite Paris-Saclay, France

Reproducible Label Chair

Adrien Krähenbühl   ICube, Université de Strasbourg, France

Program Committee

Pablo Arias   CMLA ENS Paris-Saclay, France
Fabien Baldacci   LaBRI, University of Bordeaux, France
K. Joost Batenburg   University of Antwerp, Belgium
Jenny Benois-Pineau   LaBRI, University of Bordeaux, France
Partha Bhowmick   IIT, Kharagpur, India
Arindam Biswas   IIEST, Shibpur, India
Alexandre Boulch   ONERA, France
Luc Brun   GREYC, Caen Normandy University, France
Leszek J. Chmielewski   Warsaw University of Life Sciences, Poland
Miguel Colom   CMLA ENS Paris-Saclay, France
David Coeurjolly   LIRIS, CNRS, France
Isabelle Debled-Rennesson   LORIA, University of Lorraine, France
Pascal Desbarats   LaBRI, University of Bordeaux, France
Philippe Even   LORIA, University of Lorraine, France
Yukiko Kenmochi   LIGM, CNRS, France
Bertrand Kerautret   LIRIS, Université de Lyon 2, France
Adrien Krähenbühl   ICube, Université de Strasbourg, France
Jacques-Olivier Lachaud   LAMA, University Savoie Mont Blanc, France
Bart Lamiroy   LORIA, University of Lorraine, France
Daniel Lopresti   CSE, Lehigh University, USA
Vincent Mazet   ICube, Université de Strasbourg, France
Loïc Mazo   ICube, Université de Strasbourg, France
Enric Meinhardt-Llopis   CMLA ENS Paris-Saclay, France
Nicolas Mellado   UPS, IRIT, CNRS, Université de Toulouse, France

Pascal Monasse	LIGM, École des Ponts, France
Nelson Monzón López	CTIM, ULPGC, Spain
Jean-Michel Morel	CMLA ENS Paris-Saclay, France
Pierre Moulon	Zillow Group, Seattle, USA
Khadija Musayeva	LORIA, University of Lorraine, France
Benoît Naegel	ICube, Université de Strasbourg, France
Phuc Ngo	LORIA, University of Lorraine, France
Thanh Phuong Nguyen	University of Toulon, France
Nicolas Normand	Polytech Nantes, France
Nicolas Passat	Université de Reims Champagne-Ardenne, France
Fabien Pierre	LORIA, University of Lorraine, France
Francois Rousseau	Télécom Bretagne, France
Loïc Simon	GREYC, Caen Normandy University, France
Isabelle Sivignon	GIPSA-lab, CNRS, France
Robin Strand	Centre for Image Analysis, Uppsala, Sweden
Hugues Talbot	CentraleSupelec, Université Paris-Saclay, France
Antoine Vacavant	IP/Université Clermont Auvergne, France
Jonathan Weber	MIPS, Université de Haute-Alsace, France
Laurent Wendling	LIPADE, Université Paris Descartes, France

Contents

Invited Reproducible Research Contributions

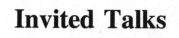

Invited Talks

Extending IPOL to New Data Types and Machine-Learning Applications

Miguel Colom[✉]

Centre de mathématiques et de leurs applications, CNRS, ENS Paris-Saclay,
Université Paris-Saclay, 94235 Cachan cedex, France
`colom@cmla.ens-cachan.fr`

Abstract. Image Processing On Line (IPOL) is a journal focused on mathematical descriptions of image processing (IP)/computer vision (CV) algorithms. Since the first article was published in 2010, it has started to become clear that the IP/CV discipline is mainly multidisciplinary. For example, nowadays images are de-noised using convolutional neural networks (CNN), and fields such as neurophysiology need of the rudiments and techniques of IP/CV, general signal processing and artificial intelligence. IPOL wants to extend the capabilities of its demo system to cope with these needs. Specifically, in this article we review the state of the current demo system and its limitations. It enunciates a detailed project on how to build a more adapted system, and its minimal requirements: new data types, problematic heterogeneous data, the pre-processing and standardization, the possibility to chain different algorithms in a complex chain, and how to compare them.

1 Introduction

Image Processing on Line (IPOL) is a research journal founded in 2010 on Reproducible Research in the field of Signal Processing (mainly Image Processing, but also video, 3D pointclouds/meshes, and audio), giving a special emphasis on the role of mathematics in the design of the algorithms [1].

As pointed by Donoho et al. [2], there is a crisis of scientific credibility since in many published papers it is not possible for the readers to reproduce exactly the same results given by the authors. The causes are many, including incomplete descriptions in the manuscripts, not releasing the source code, or that the published algorithm does not correspond to what actually is implemented. Each IPOL article has an online demo associated which allows users to run the algorithms with their own data; the reviewers of the IPOL articles must carefully check that both the description and the implementation match.

Since it started in 2010, the IPOL demo system has been continuously improved and according to usage statistics collected along these years, it has about 250 unique visitors per day. However, several problems of design and potential improvement actions were identified and it was decided to build a second version of the system based on microservices [3].

© Springer Nature Switzerland AG 2019
B. Kerautret et al. (Eds.): RRPR 2018, LNCS 11455, pp. 3–24, 2019.
https://doi.org/10.1007/978-3-030-23987-9_1

The full redesign of the demo system proposed in the project will not only solve the problems enumerated before, but will allow also to expand IPOL to much more complex data types and thus to new applications. In particular, we are especially interested in multidimensional signals since they have applications in physiological analysis (data from accelerometers, oculometry, EGC, EMG, EEG), as well as mixtures of data types (for example, time-series signals along with text).

Another important extension of IPOL will be to allow Machine Learning applications. Specifically, to allow the algorithms to be able to explore the set of experiments performed by the users as training data. A typical task which can be learned is the choice of the best parameters to run the algorithm according to the characteristics of the input data. For example, in the case of images the values of the parameters needed to segment a hyperspectral image in general depend on the number of channels and other parameters on the image which could be learned automatically by the system. In the case of Machine Learning algorithms, the space of hyperparameters can vary from a few of them (up to ten for the main Machine Learning algorithms) to millions in the case of deep learning applications. The choice of the hyperparameters is an open question under intensive research[1] and the interest of a learning step to automatically choose the best parameters is clear.

Machine Learning algorithms require important changes in the architecture of the IPOL system to allow not only new data types, but also adding pre-processing steps, optimal data storage to allow fast queries, management of databases, and comparison of algorithms. The system will also require training processes which run continuously and explore the contents of the archive of experiments.

After the first four years of publications, the problems noted before were detected [4] and the architecture of the system was redesigned by a group of volunteers and part-time collaborators. We arrived at a working prototype of a new demo system which is scalable, easy to debug, and which implements the automatic generation of demos, thus alleviating the work load of the editor and thus allowing for fast demo publishing. Section 2 discusses the design of this preliminary system. Section 3 presents the plan to extend IPOL to a wide-purpose platform which allows to run algorithms with much more complex data types and multiple application fields (medical, research, industrial).

Section 4 discusses the business model of this new platform, and presents a plan to recover the investment and make the project auto-sustainable, with an estimation of the costs. Finally Sect. 5 concludes this article.

2   The Current (New) System

In 2014 we identified [4] several technical problems related to the architecture of the demo system, including the lack of modularity, tightly-coupled interfaces,

---

[1] See for example Cedric Malherbe's PhD dissertation: http://www.theses.fr/s144139.

difficulties to share the computational load along different machines, or complicated debugging of the system in case of malfunction. We found also editorial problems, such as the slow and rigid procedure that the editors needed to follow to create or modify demos.

After a careful analysis of the system and with the knowledge accumulated in those first years, we decided that the best option was to move to a more flexible architecture oriented to (micro)services (Sect. 2.1). We understood that the slow process to create and edit demos was a bottleneck in the first version of the demo system and thus we decided to create an abstract specification for the demos (the Demo Description Lines, or *DDL*) to allow automatic and fast demo generation (Sect. 2.2). And since we needed to have a tool which could be used by non-technical editors, we created a graphical web interface to create and edit demos, as well as the associated data, the Control Panel (Sect. 2.3).

After the improvements in the system, we have now:

- A function architecture of microservices, with 7 modules
- Fast demo creation. The new system accounts at this moment for 39 published demos, 6 pre-prints, and 72 workshops. The fact that there is a large number of workshops compared to the publications confirms that now it is easy and fast for our editors to create new demos
- Video demos
- Audio demos
- Interactive controls almost finished. They will be ready in a few weeks.
- The possibility to add custom Javascript code to the demos for editors with special requirements, without complexifying the demo system itself
- A system easier to debug when a bug is detected. Now it is really easy to track down bugs, since every module has its own logging system and automatic alerts. At this moment there are no known bugs in the system, and if they appeared they would be detect, the engineers warned, and fixed immediately.

Adding completely new features such as support for machine learning applications with a training step will require intense engineering efforts and more engineers in the team to build it in a reasonable time.

2.1   The IPOL Demo System Architecture

The architecture of the new IPOL demo system is an Service-Oriented Architecture (SOA) based on microservices[2]. This change was motivated by the problems found in the previous version of the demo system. First, it was designed as a monolithic program[3] which made it quite easy to deploy in the servers and to run it locally, but at the cost of many disadvantages. Given that it was a monolithic system, it was difficult to split it into different machines to share the computational load of the algorithms being executed. A simple solution would be to create specialized units to run the algorithms and to call them from the

---

[2] We use Python 3 but in fact the microservices may be written in any language.

[3] Of course, with a good separation of functionality among different classes.

monolithic code, but this clearly evokes the first step to move to a microservices architecture. Indeed, this first step of *breaking the monolith* [3] can be iterated until all the functions of the system have been delegated in different modules. In the case of IPOL, we created specialized modules and removed the code from the monolith until the very monolith became a module itself: Core. This Core module is in charge of all the system and delegates the operations to other modules. Figure 1 summarizes the IPOL modules and other components in the architecture of the system.

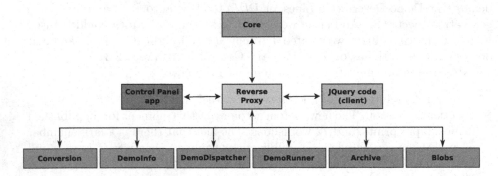

Fig. 1. Modular architecture of the current IPOL demo system.

Other problems we had in the previous version of the demo system got solved when we moved to the microservices architecture. Since there is a loose coupling between Core and the other modules (in the sense that they are independent programs which communicate via an HTTP API), different members of the development team can work at the same time without worrying about the implementation details or data structures used in other parts of the system. Also, tracking down malfunctions is easier: since Core centralizes all the operations, when a bug shows it can only be generated either at Core or at the involved module, but not at any other part of the system. In the old system a bug could be caused by complex conditions which depend on the global state of the program, making debugging a complex task. And as noted before, the fact that the architecture of the system is distributed and modular by design makes it very natural and simple to have mechanisms to share the computational load among several machines.

Hiding the internal implementation details behind the interfaces of the modules is an essential part of the system, and it is needed to provide loose coupling between its components. The internal architecture of the system is of course hidden from the users when they interact with the system, but it is also hidden *from the inside*. This means that any module (Core included) does not need to know the location of the modules. Instead, all of them use a published API.

Once the API is defined, the routing to the modules is implemented by a reverse proxy[4]. It receives the requests from the clients according to this pattern: /api/<module>/<service> and redirects them to the corresponding module. Figure 2 shows how the API messages received by the proxy are routed to the corresponding modules, thus hiding the internal architecture of the system.

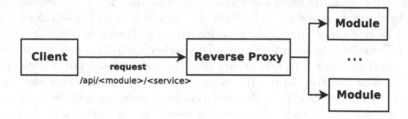

Fig. 2. The reverse proxy routes the API messages to the corresponding modules.

Modules: The IPOL demo system is made of several standalone units used by the Core module to delegate specialized and well isolated functions. This section describes briefly these microservices modules.

Blobs (Binary Large OBjects): each demo of IPOL offers the user a set of default blobs which can be tagged and linked to different demos. Thus, the users are not forced to supply their own files for the execution of the algorithms. The term *blob* in IPOL refers to any file that can be used as an input, regardless its type. In an image-processing demo they would be images, but they can be also videos, or even text files representing physiological signals, for instance. The system does not need to know their particular type since the execution flow is always the same (load inputs, eventually convert them, run the algorithm, store the results in the archive, and show results). Only when needed (for example, when the Conversion module needs to perform some kind of transformation in the data) the corresponding module will request its actual type. This module introduces the concept of *templates*, which are sets of blobs which can be associated to a particular demo. For example, this allows all the demos of a specific type (e.g., de-noising) to share the same images as default input data. Instead of editing each demo one by one, the editors can simply edit their template to make changes in all the demos, and then particular changes to each specific demo.

Archive: the Archive module stores all the experiments performed by the IPOL with their original data. The database stores the experiments and blobs, which are related with a junction table with a many-to-many relationship. It is worth noting that the system does not store duplicates of the same blob, but detects them from their SHA1 hash.

This module offers several services, such as adding (or deleting) an experiment or deleting all the set of experiments related to a particular demo. The

---

[4] We use Nginx as the reverse proxy.

archive also has services to show particular experiments or several pages with all the experiments stored since the first use of the archive.

Core: this module is the centralized controller of the whole IPOL system. It delegates most of the tasks to the other modules, such as the execution of the demos, archiving experiments, or retrieving metadata, among others.

When an execution is requested, it obtains first the textual description of the corresponding demo by using the DDL from DemoInfo and it copies the blobs chosen by the users as the algorithm's input. Then, it asks for the workload of the different DemoRunners and gives this information to Dispatcher in order to pick the best DemoRunner according to the Dispatcher's selection policy. Core asks the chosen DemoRunner to first ensure that the source codes are well compiled in the machine and then to run the algorithm with the parameters and inputs set by the user. Core waits until the execution has finished or a timeout happens. Finally, it delegates to Archive to store the results of the experiment. In case of any failures, Core terminates the execution and stores the errors in its log file. Eventually, it will send warning emails to the technical staff of IPOL (internal error) or to the IPOL editors of the article (compilation or execution failure).

Dispatcher: in order to distribute the computational load along different machines, this module is responsible of assigning a concrete DemoRunner according to a configurable policy. The policy takes into account the requirements of a demo and the workload of all DemoRunners and returns the one which fits best. The DemoRunners and their workloads are provided by Core. Figure 3 shows the communication between Core, Dispatcher, and the DemoRunner modules.

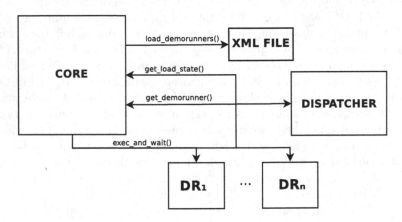

Fig. 3. Communication between Core, Dispatcher, and the DemoRunner modules.

Currently Dispatcher implements three policies:

– **random:** it assigns a random DemoRunner
– **sequential:** it iterates sequentially the list of DemoRunners;
– **lowest workload:** it chooses the DemoRunner with the lowest workload.

The choice of the actual policy is a configuration option in the module. It can be changed by the system operators at any moment, but the module can not change the policy depending on the execution needs of the system so far.

Any policy selects only those DemoRunners that satisfy the requirements (for example, having MATLAB installed, or a particular version of openCV).

DemoInfo: the DemoInfo module stores the metadata of the demos. For example, the title, abstract, ID, or its authors, among others. It also stores the abstract textual description of the demo (DDL). All this information can be required by Core when executing a demo or by the Control Panel when the demo is edited with its website interface.

It is possible that the demo requires non-reviewed support code to show results. In this case, the demo can use custom scripts to create result plots. Note that this only refers to scripts and data which is not peer-reviewed. In case they are important to reproduce the results or figures in the article, they need to be in the peer-reviewed source code package.

DemoRunner: this module controls the execution of the IPOL demos. The DemoRunner module is responsible of informing Core about the load of the machine where it is running, of ensuring that the demo execution is done with the last source codes provided by the authors (it downloads and compiles these codes to maintain them updated), and of executing the algorithm with the parameters set by the users. It takes care of stopping the demo execution if a timeout is reached, and to inform Core about the causes of a demo execution failure so Core can take the best action in response. In order to distribute and share the computational load of the whole system, several demoRunner instances can be deployed on different machines. Each of the instances can declare different capabilities, as for example being able to run MATLAB code, of the presence of a GPU.

2.2   Automatic Demo Generation

In the previous version of the IPOL demo system the demo editors had to write Python code to create a new demo. Specifically, to override some methods in a base demo class in order to configure its input parameters, to call the program implementing the algorithm, and also to design Mako HTML templates for the results page.

This approach does not really solve anything, and it simply passes the problem (the inability of the system to generate demos from a simple textual description) to the hands of the demo editors, that are forced to write code and HTML templates. Of course, these are the kind of tasks that can be automated and should not be made by human editors.

When Python code was written by the demo editors, it was prone to bugs which are specific to each demo. Moreover, fixing a bug in a particular demo does not guarantee that the same solution as-is could be applied to other demos with the same problem. Indeed, different demo editors might have written different codes in each demo to solve the same problem.

In fact, it is evident that this design can be simplified and the tasks automated. Indeed, to completely define a demo all one needs is:

1. The title of the demo;
2. the URL where the system should download the source code of the demo;
3. the compilation instructions;
4. the type interaction of the user with the demo (for example, drawing segments over the image, or annotating an input signal, or simply picking one image);
5. the input parameters along with their type and default values;
6. a description of what needs to be shown as results.

This information is not tied to any particular language or visualization technique, but it can be a simple abstract textual description. In IPOL we called this abstract textual description the Demo Description Lines (DDL). The IPOL editors only need to write such a description and the system takes care of making available the demo according to it. This not only avoids any coding problems (since there is nothing to code, but writing the corresponding DDL), but also allows IPOL to have non-expert demo editors, and makes it possible to edit and publish demos quickly. As an example, Fig. 4 shows the graphical tool used to edit the DDL of a demo within the Control Panel tool.

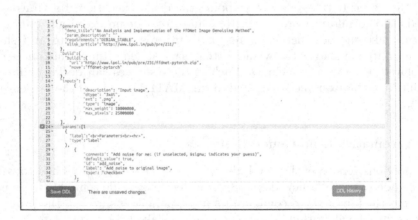

Fig. 4. Graphical tool to edit the DDL of a demo in the Control Panel.

2.3   Editorial Management: The Control Panel

The Control Panel is a web application which offers a unified interface to configure and manage the platform, intended for non-technical editors. It allows to create/modify/delete the list of IPOL editors, the demos along their textual descriptions, upload new testing dataset, and to customize the demos with extra code for advanced users who need it. It allows also editors to remove specific experiments upon request (for example, in the case of copyright images) or if

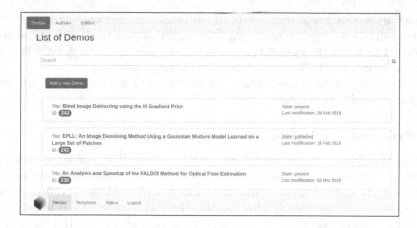

Fig. 5. List of demos as shown in the Control Panel.

inappropriate content is found. Figure 5 shows a screenshot of the Control Panel application as shown in the browser.

Even if it is an internal tool for the journal management, it has been designed with these main objectives:

– To allow fast and easy demo creation and edition, to avoid that the generation of demos becomes a bottleneck. The DDL description was created in the new system to this purpose (see Sect. 2.2).
– To incorporate as many editors as possible to the journal. To achieve this objective the Control Panel needs to be a tool intended for editors without no special technical background. All the technical system administration tools are outside the Control Panel.
– To hide the complexity of the distributed system to the editor. Indeed, IPOL is a complex system running in several machines, but from the point of view of the editors and the demo users they simply interact with a web page front-end.

3   Plan to Extend to a Wide-Purpose Platform

IPOL has been evolving since it was funded in 2010, from a very simple demo system which required the editors to write actual Python code and design HTML templates, to a system of a distributed system started in 2015 with load balancing along several machines and automatic demo generation from an abstract description syntax.

The next step is first to move to new data types (audio, video, 3D) and finally to allow different applications, including Machine Learning. Adapting the system to a wide-purpose platform will require some changes in the architecture of the system (new modules) and better data organization (Archive, mainly) but still the current modular architecture of the system will be able to support it. In any case, moving to new application fields and at the same time keeping a generalist platform will require strong engineering efforts and a stable team with permanent positions. This is not the case at this moment, and we need to work on this point to be able to extend IPOL with advanced features reliably.

The following sections present and discuss the steps needed to build the next evolution of the IPOL system.

3.1   Extended Architecture: Support for Applications

There is a fundamental difference between the current IPOL demo system and the complete platform offering Software as a Service (SaaS) applications and learning capabilities: their execution time. The complete platform differs from a demo system in the fact that it allows applications whose lifetime[5] is largely over the short period of execution of a demo. In the case of a demo the input data is loaded, the algorithm executed, the results shown, and the demo has totally finished. In the case of algorithms which can learn from the archive, they need to be running indefinitely. Once they are run, they can receive events indicating the there is new data in the archive, or to explore it regularly.

We shall call these new processes with a large lifetime *Applications*. The system will have two different kinds of processes:

– Demos
– Applications

Nevertheless, the architecture of the new system needs not be redesigned in order to have these new functionalities, but new modules need to be added and they will share information within the system.

The first module which needs to be added is the equivalent to Core which delegates the demo operations along different specialized modules, but for the Applications. We will call this new module *AppCore* and rename the existing one to *DemoCore*.

The DemoCore will delegate some specialized functions in already existing modules, for example in Conversion or Blobs since they still be needed in the context of the applications. But new modules will be exclusive to AppCore, such as:

– *Databases*: storage and management of training and testing datasets
– *UserAccess*: lists of users and authorization management

The same way DemoCore offers an API of microservices that the web application uses to render demos in the client's browser, AppCore will offer microservices to be used by external applications. We can think for example of a MATLAB application or a Jupyter notebook which uses the AppCore's services to log in and then visualize classification results obtained using the corresponding learning databases. Figure 6 shows the architecture of the complete platform.

---

[5] Here we refer to the "wall clock time" of the process, not their CPU usage time. The application is expected to have a large lifetime when most of the time the process in idle, whereas in the case of a demo the process is CPU intensive.

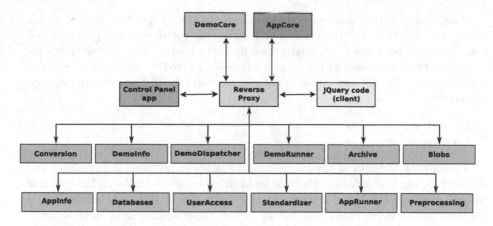

Fig. 6. The complete modular architecture of the future IPOL platform.

Note that the platform is not tied to a particular visualization tool (say, a website) or to any specific framework (MATLAB, R, or the Android system, for example) but instead it offers generic webservices that can be used with them. This way the platform remains generic but at the same time it can be customized with the frameworks preferred by its users.

3.2 Extension to New Data Types

The new architecture of the IPOL demo system (Sect. 2) already allows to work with arbitrary data types. By design, we chose to refer to the data generically as *blobs*, instead of being attached to a particular data type such as images and others. The system manages the data in terms of blobs, and only a particular module ("Conversion") (see Fig. 1) needs to know about the actual details of the type to make conversions. This means that when adding a new data type only Conversion needs to be modified whereas the rest of the system modules remain the same.

The execution flow given an input blob is the following:

1. The blob arrives to Core module. The origin can be either one of the input blobs offered by the demo or a new blob uploaded by the user.
2. Core examines the DDL to check if the demo authorizes data conversion and also it that conversion is actually needed. For example: reduce an image to the maximum allowed size and convert from JPEG to PNG.
3. In case the modification is authorized and needed, Core delegates the conversion of the blob to Conversion.
4. The Conversion module converts the blob to meet the requirements written at the DDL. Only in the context of Conversion the actual data type is taken into account. Outside it is only a generic *blob*.
5. Core goes on with the execution of the algorithm. With the original blob or with the converted.

The kind of conversions needed depend on the data type. For images, audio, video, and 3D they are basically two: resampling (or decimation) and format conversion. Other data types might need different and specific transformations.

While the conversion of the data itself is supported by the current system, depending on the application it might not be enough. Indeed, two more steps are needed:

– Data standardization
– Pre-processing

Given that the aim of the platform is to support multiple applications and data types, the input data is likely to be in different file formats and in different ranges. We can think for example in the data of two different accelerometer sensors: one of them could give values of the three spatial axes in m/s units, while the other might give only two of the three axes in cm/s. Before attempting the process the data, the system needs to put the input data in a common format.

Even if the data has been standardized, it might require pre-processing. For example, an algorithm might not work with missing ("NA" - Not Available) values, while for others this could be acceptable. The system might decide to pre-process the data in order to remove NA samples by interpolation, or simply to remove them before passing the data to the algorithm for execution.

The solution is to add two new modules to the system:

– *Standardizer*: to structure the data in a format understood by the system and the algorithms;
– *Preprocessing*: to perform pre-processing steps before execution according to the needs of the algorithm.

Core would systematically pass the data to these two modules to check if these steps are needed and to actually perform them in that case.

About the web interface, it needs to be expanded to support the visualization of the new data types. At the moment of writing this text, the system has full support for video processing and visualization and the interactive controls (masks for inpainting demos, points for Poisson editing, segments for lens correction, etc.) are expected to be finished in a few weeks. Figure 7 shows the IPOL demo of the published article *Ball Pivoting Algorithm* for which the system shows the result with a 3D mesh renderer.

3.3   Comparison of Algorithms

A desired feature in the future platform is the comparison of algorithms. At this moment every demo is an isolated unit which takes the input data, applies an algorithm with the configured parameters, and finally shows the results. However, being able to measure the performance of the algorithms is of great interest it this would allow to score them and to know which is the best parameter choice according to the algorithm and the input data.

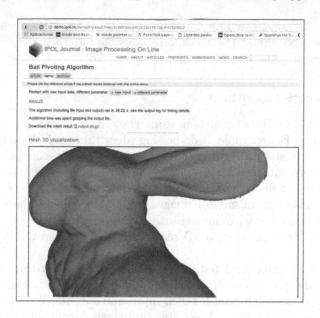

Fig. 7. IPOL demo of the published article *Ball Pivoting Algorithm* showing the results with a 3D mesh renderer.

In order to compare the algorithms a metric of quality must be available. This metric can depend solely in the results (for example, exploiting structural similarity in the case of images [5]) or a metric with respect to a given ground-truth.

The inputs and outputs of the algorithm might vary largely and therefore we need to define common data formats in the platform. Clearly, to compare two algorithms their outputs need to be encoded with compatible formats to allow automatic comparisons.

The role of Preprocessing Standardizer presented in Sect. 3.2 becomes clear here. Indeed, the comparison of algorithms feature relies on this two modules since the platform needs to:

- Define formats to homogenize the outputs of diverse algorithms. The Standardizer module will be the responsible for this task, delegated from the DemoCore or AppDemo controller modules.
- In the case of missing data or if pre-processing is needed, then Preprocessing will be invoked too.

Sometimes it will be needed to express the same data in different forms. For example, some metrics would need a temporal series while others could work only with their spectra. The role of Standardizer is to put the data in a flexible format when it is entered into the platform for the first time, not to perform data format conversions during execution (which is a different task and performed by Conversion, see Fig. 6).

The platform needs to provide large datasets to test the algorithms with and also several metrics to perform the comparisons. In the most favorable scenario, these datasets are previously annotated by experts and serve as a ground-truth to evaluate the algorithms. The module responsible for storing the testing and learning databases is the Databases module (Sect. 3.5).

3.4   Chaining of Algorithms

The *chaining* of algorithms consists in using the output of one algorithm as the input for another. For example, a de-noising algorithm could be applied to an input image before attempting object recognition. Another example may be an algorithm to interpolate missing samples in the data acquired from an accelerometer could be run in a first step before trying to determine the trajectory followed by the sensor. In the case of satellite images, we could think of a chain which first de-noises pairs of images with one algorithm, then rectifies them with a second algorithm, and finally performs a 3D reconstruction with yet another different algorithm.

This problem is utterly related to the comparison of algorithms sketched in Sect. 3.3, since the key to be able to connect one algorithm with a different one is that both have a common format for their input and outputs. The platform needs to define general formats for each possible input and output for the algorithm.

Some general data types that should be defined within the platform according to the current editorial needs:

- Temporal series of k dimensions, allowing missing values.
- Sets of points in a 3D point cloud. In general, sets of hyperpoints with an arbitrary number of points.
- Sets of edges and vertices to define 3D meshes. In general, edges and vertices defined in a hyperspace.
- Images and Video. In general, k-dimensional hypercubes of data.

Other generic formats might be defined according to the evolution of the platform and the needs of the users.

We propose to create input/output wrappers in the algorithms to adapt the data to the formats of the platform, to avoid forcing the implemented algorithm to follow specific formats. This way the platform would allow most of the algorithms available without the need of adapting them.

In the future system a final result might not come only from the execution of a single algorithm, but built from the concatenation of many.

3.5   Machine Learning Applications

Machine Learning algorithms have an extra step which makes them different to most of the Signal Processing algorithms: a first training step. Indeed, they normally proceed in three different phases:

1. A training (or *learning*) step with some examples and one or more metrics to evaluate the performance of the algorithm. For example, a neural network

classifier intended for face recognition needs to be trained with many samples previously labeled as faces and non-faces. Typically the learning step is slow, requires many samples, and can be improved by adding more samples to the learning database.

2. A validation step, to ensure that the training is not biased.
3. Prediction. Once the algorithm has already learned according to the training samples (say, a neural network with well-adjusted weights or a SVM[6] classifier with the right hyperplane) it can proceed to predict the result given a sample that the algorithm has not seen before.

On the other hand, the assessment phase needs:

1. A metric (i.e. a formula), which typically is different from the metric used during training.
2. A test set, different from the training set.

The two-step process described above might not be directly applicable when the training of the neural network needs a complex customized training and therefore can not be reduced to uploading learning data and applying standard stochastic optimization. Also, depending on the application the learning step could consist on several phases.

For those complex cases we expect the learning to be performed offline and to work with two types of data:

– The learning set that must be kept for records and
– the generated neural network.

The researcher should upload a script (as *demoExtras*, see Sect. 3.6) governing the learning, in addition to data and to the back-propagation codes. In order to make it reproducible it would be needed that all the details on the training process are documented, including any random seeds, the hyperparameters, the initialization of the weights when learning (for example, Xavier's initialization), number of mini-batches, and in general any other learning parameters which are relevant to reproduce the same results.

The typical demos in the current IPOL system are not well adapted to this new schema since their cycle is simple to read the input data, apply some algorithm with the given parameters, and finally show the results. It is possible however to give some pre-learned databases, but the new platform will be able to update its own training datasets according to the input data from authorized users.

Let us present a typical case of use of the platform. In order to make it more understandable, we will explain it in a concrete application such as healthcare.

The platform will be used by persons with different roles, such as clinicians, technicians, and researchers from different fields (for example, physiologists, signal processing researchers, statisticians, expert systems researchers, etc). Their diverse interests converge at the platform. Doctors are mostly interested in

---

[6] Support Vector Machine.

obtaining relevant information after they have introduced data of a particular patient (for example, the possibility of discovering a neurological problem from the analysis of saccadic signatures in ocular movements [6]), as well as tracking the evolution of a patient over time.

One of the objectives of the platform is to obtain substantial results by applying Machine Learning algorithms. In this example our aim would be helping clinicians extract relevant medical information from large and multidimensional datasets.

Doctors will decide if the data of their patients (after mandatory anonymization [7]) can be incorporated to the databases of the platform, or not. For example, if the clinician has labeled data it can be used as a ground-truth for many algorithms of the platform and thus over colleagues benefit from it. Or they can decide not to share but still use it as a tool with their own data.

Not all users will be authorized to upload training data (or at least, it needs to be peer-reviewed first), since the performance of the platform relies on the quality of its learning base and thus it needs to be carefully controlled. Thus, depending on the role of the users there will be several combinations of rights and authorization levels: possibility of uploading training data, possibility of executing the algorithms on uploaded test data, possibility to label an already existent dataset, possibility of creating groups of users with common right for certain datasets, etc. Instead of fixing the set of possibilities it is better to leave them open as configurable options and to set up rights for users or groups of users depending on their roles. As advanced in Sect. 3.1, the platform will use a new *Databases* module to store and manage the permissions for the training and test datasets.

In order to take advantage of both the practitioners' extended knowledge and the presence of numerous healthcare datasets, the platform could also include a crowdsourcing aspect (see e.g. [8]). Using trained classification or scoring algorithms, unlabelled data with the largest amount of uncertainty could be presented to the platform medical user for additional input – thus both improving the quality of the dataset, the performance of the algorithm, and presenting practitioner with interesting usecases.

In the case of executing an algorithm with a test dataset (say, to perform prediction), the execution will be similar to a typical IPOL demo. It can be sketched as follows:

1. The users upload or choose one of their datasets;
2. they chain several algorithms and configure their parameters;
3. the algorithm is run. The user can wait until it finishes, or it can be stored and recovered later;
4. the results are shown;
5. the results are archived for further analysis.

This is a complex interaction, perhaps for the most advanced users. However, most users (say, medical doctors) would just upload their data and wait for their automatic results. However, the system needs of course to be designed such a way that it copes with both the complex and common cases.

Technically, the request arrives to Core, which delegates the selection of the most available DemoRunner for the execution, DemoRunner will perform the execution, and then Core will retrieve the results. Finally, Core will send a command to Archive to store all relevant information on the experiment. See Fig. 3.

While the current system could support easily Machine Learning learning algorithm to perform *testing* (say, classification or prediction), it needs to be extended to reach the new architecture depicted in Fig. 6). Indeed, as explained in Sect. 3.1, the execution cycle of a simple demo does not allow to have a long learning phase.

This operative does not adapt well to the needed learning phase and thus a new entity (the *applications*). The applications are processes which are started by AppCore and instead of finishing after a fixed period has elapsed, they simply enter in a *sleep* mode. They can be woken up by AppCore for several reasons, as for example when new data arrives to Archive, or they can wake up by themselves at regular intervals to perform learning on the data available in the platform.

To better understand the concept of the applications, let us think of an algorithm to detect faces in pictures using an SVM. The users will upload their own pictures to the demo to check if the system is able to detect or not the faces that might be present in the image. The users will provide feedback about if the system managed to detect a face in the right position (positive), or if it detected a face in a place where it was not any (false positive), or if it missed an actual face (false negative). To do it, the demo could use an SVM classifier whose hyperplane is shaped according to a learning step. Thus, the published algorithm will implement two tasks: testing (used by the demo), and training (performed by the application). We can imagine the algorithm's package as a ZIP file with two folders with independent codes, one for testing and the other for training.

Once the algorithm has been installed in the system, AppCore will start the corresponding application which uses the training code. It will wake up regularly the application with an event indicating that it has new feedback, and then the application will run the training code to update the SVM hyperplane. This will improve the performance of the demo. Once the training with the new data has finished the application will enter in a sleep mode until it is woken up by AppCore again.

Note that when we write *the AppRunner* or *the DemoRunner* modules, actually we refer to an instance of many of them. Indeed, while the other modules are unique in the system, the runners are many distributed processes. Each time Core needs to execute a process (say, a demo or a learning phase), it uses Dispatcher module to pick a particular runner and send the execution. For example, in the current system we have three distributed demoRunners available. One is physically installed at CMLA laboratory, and the other two are in the installations of an external provider. This is easily configured with simple configuration files.

In the case of the applications they will be also distributed along several servers. The AppCore will ask Dispatcher for an AppRunner, then AppCore will wake the runner up and ask to update its learning database when needed. Note that AppCore has the possibility of running several instances of the same learning process along different runners if necessary. For example, it can split the input data into several batches and make different runners process each of the parts at the same time.

Apart of adding these new AppCore and AppRunner modules to the architecture of the system, the existing Archive module will be improved to allow queries and receive structured information quickly. For example, we can think in a demo that runs a classification algorithm in images (let's say, it tells which is the animal in the image). If the demo configures Archive to store extra information about the inputs (say, level of JPEG compression, the mean intensity of the image, ...), it would be possible to extract meaningful information afterwards. For example, it how relevant is the compression level of the image when performing classification, or how images with very low contrast or saturated impact the performance. This could be done with a query language very similar to SQL.

Improving Archive will allow not only Machine Learning applications, but also for more complex Signal Processing algorithms in the demo system.

Finally, already existing Control Panel (Sect. 3.6) will be extended to allow the system operators to manage[7] the installed applications.

3.6   System Management with a Unified Tool

A tool to allow non-technical administrators to manage the platform is needed. Such a tool is known as the *Control Panel* in the current system (see Sect. 2.3).

The Control Panel allows the IPOL editors to create new demos and modify any existing demos. This tool is a web application where the editors have access after typing their username and password and one of the design requirements is that it should be used by editors without any technical background. It allows however to add extra code to the demos (known as *demoExtras*) in order that advanced editors can customize them but nevertheless most of the demos are defined from a simple textual description (see Sect. 2.2).

In order to allow the complete system with the extensions presented, the Control Panel also needs to be completed. Specifically, it needs new sections to:

- Install, configure, and remove Applications, in a similar way to what does already for the demos.
- Create, edit, and remove users.
- Add, remove, and configure the access right of the learning and testing databases for each user or group of users according to their roles in the platform.

---

[7] Add, remove, start, stop, and configure user database rights.

The existence of a unified tool such as the Control Panel[8] and the use of an API (see Sect. 2.1) to interact with the system hides not only the implementation details but also the fact that the system is distributed along different machines. Indeed, the editors manage the system with a simple tool which hides all its complexity and lets them configure it quickly and easily.

4 Business Model: The IPOL Case

This section discusses briefly about the business model that RR platforms could adopt, focusing on the experience that the authors have as editors of the IPOL journal.

The scientific interest of IPOL a platform for reproducible research is clear after look at the number of visitors (about 250 unique visits per day) and the number of citations of the published papers (see Fig. 8, total citations: 3497, h-index: 29, i10-index: 61). It has also proved its utility as a tool to prove the competence of the research group and to obtain research contracts (DxO, CNES, ONR, and others).

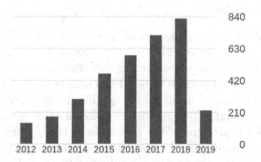

Fig. 8. IPOL citations from 2012 to 2019. Source: Google Scholar. Total citations: 3497, h-index: 29, i10-index: 61.

A very pertinent question is how to obtain a business return which ensures the sustainability of the project for the long term, out of the support of the public agencies (CNRS, ERC, and others).

A possible move would be to move to the Software as a Service (SaaS) model and to receive incomes from:

– The use of already learned databases. This model is already used by large big-data companies such as Google, for example with their TensorFlow product[9].

---

[8] Nowadays, even configuration tools like this are regarded as part of an experimental system, and techniques like A/B testing are used to improve the performance (usability) of the tool.

[9] https://cloud.google.com/products/machine-learning/.

- The use of computational services. This modality is implemented by similar platforms such as Code Ocean[10] and others.
- Consulting services. The start-up created to build the final platform will collaborate closely with the scientific staff at CMLA (professors, associate researchers, postdocs, and PhD candidates) and eventually incorporate them into the company. This way the company will not only offer the services of the platform, but also scientific consulting and advice.
- Expanding to areas other than Image Processing and Computer Vision. Indeed, in IPOL we are exploring the possibility to accept articles on more general signal processing, including physiological signals.

Other ways of receiving incomes such as crowdfunding or donations might help too. For example, the Jupyter project is funded mainly by donations[11] and GV[12] (Google Ventures) has invested in projects of companies such as Uber, Light, Slack, Periscope, and many others.

Some companies have already expressed their interest on our future platform. Other companies[13] use or have used IPOL for research purposes, with reference source codes and detailed algorithmic descriptions.

4.1   Resources Needed

IPOL began as part of the PhD project of a single person [1], and since then it has been continuously improved. First by the generous contributions of several collaborators, and finally with a group of interns and software engineers working part time or hired for short periods to build the new version of the demo system.

At this point, the project needs highly qualified engineers. It is no longer a small project but a complex system with requires a professional and dedicated team with stable positions. One of the problems at this moment is that it takes months to train a new engineer in the details of the project and most of the time they leave when they start to be really productive. The reason why the engineers leave the project even if they would like to go on is precisely the lack of stability and perspectives, since the public organizations are not able to create stable positions. When the engineers leave the project the group loses all the accumulated knowledge and again we need to train new members.

Only one person in the team has a permanent position, and even though the dedication to the project is part time.

It is important to create stable positions for the project and also to obtain funding to go on with the engineering tasks. A minimum requirement is to obtain at least one permanent position for the technical director and to have funding for a team of one director and three software engineers during two years. The current system is distributed along three servers rented from an external provided, with a cost of 400 euros/month. We estimate that the final platform will need about

---

[10] https://codeocean.com/pricing.
[11] http://jupyter.org/donate.html.
[12] https://www.gv.com/portfolio/.
[13] We could cite DxO, Thales, or Technicolor, among others.

8 servers with a cost of $400 \times 8 = 3200$ euros/month. The number of servers is flexible and can be adapted to the computational needs of the platforms at any time.

5 Conclusions

The first version of the IPOL demo system has been working since the first article was published in 2010, with a total of 152 articles, 3364 citations and h- and i10-indexes of 29 and 61 respectively. While it is clear that the system is functional, some problems were detected: the system was difficult to debug to track down malfunctions, it suffered from tightly coupled interfaces, it was complicated to distribute the computational load among different machines, and the editors needed to write Python code to create and edit demos. These problems compromised the durability of the system at the same time they started to create a bottleneck that prevented to create and edit demos quickly. These problems are already solved with the new version of the demo system, a distributed architecture of microservices, presented in Sect. 2.

Of course, even if the system is already functional it still needs strong engineering efforts before it is considered a finished product. The plan for the very short term is to integrate new data types such as video, audio, and 3D. We are quite confident on this task since the system is able to manage generic types (even if we refer to *images*, for the system they are simply *blobs*) and it will come down to a visualization problem in the website interface.

With more than one hundred published demos, more than seven years of activity, about 250 unique visitors/day, thousands of experiments performed by the users with their original data, IPOL has been proved to be a useful tool not only for research but also as a value-added tool for the industry.

The existence of similar initiatives such as Jupyter, Code Ocean, RunMy-Code, and openCV indicate a great interest of the scientific community and the industry for this kind of platforms, for which IPOL is a clear precursor. These other platforms do not need to be understood as a threat for IPOL, but instead as an indication of the market trend. We refer the reader to [9] for a comparison and discussion on platforms that might be used to implement reproducible research. Nevertheless, IPOL needs to go a step beyond and move from a demo system to a wide-scope platform to build complete applications over it, following the Software as a Service model. Machine learning algorithms, the use of learning databases, and the ability of the platform to improve these databases is a unique business that is worth exploiting.

As explained in Sect. 4.1, while the technical competence is already met and a working system has already been built, it is fundamental for the project to have a stable team. We can afford some temporal contributors (say, interns and engineers hired for specific tasks), but the fact that nobody in the team has a permanent position (not even the technical director) puts the continuity the whole project in obvious danger.

Without any doubt, this is an ambitious project but nevertheless realistic, and the fact that it has been running for almost ten years already is the best proof of feasibility.

Acknowledgments. I would like to thank Jean-Michel Morel, Nicolas Vayatis, Bertrand Kerautret, and Daniel Lopresti for their valuable comments that helped improve this work.

References

1. Limare, N.: Reproducible Research, Software Quality, Online Interfaces and Publishing for Image Processing. Ph.D. thesis, École Normale Supérieure de Cachan (2012)
2. Donoho, D.L., Maleki, A., Rahman, I.U., Shahram, M., Stodden, V.: Reproducible research in computational harmonic analysis. Comput. Sci. Eng. **11**, 8–18 (2009)
3. Neuman, S.: Building Microservices: Designing Fine-Grained Systems. O'Reilly Media, Sebastopol (2015)
4. Colom, M., Kerautret, B., Limare, N., Monasse, P., Morel, J.M.: IPOL: a new journal for fully reproducible research; analysis of four years development. In: 2015 7th International Conference on New Technologies, Mobility and Security (NTMS), pp. 1–5. IEEE (2015)
5. Wang, Z., Bovik, A.C., Sheikh, H.R., Simoncelli, E.P.: Image quality assessment: from error visibility to structural similarity. IEEE Trans. Image Process. **13**, 600–612 (2004)
6. Purves, D., Augustine, G., Fitzpatrick, D.: Neural Control of Saccadic Eye Movements. Sinauer Associates, Sunderland (2001)
7. Neubauer, T., Heurix, J.: A methodology for the pseudonymization of medical data. Int. J. Med. Inform. **80**, 190–204 (2011)
8. Foncubierta Rodríguez, A., Müller, H.: Ground truth generation in medical imaging: a crowdsourcing-based iterative approach. In: Proceedings of the ACM Multimedia 2012 Workshop on Crowdsourcing for Multimedia, pp. 9–14. ACM (2012)
9. Colom, M., Kerautret, B.: An Overview of Platforms for Reproducible Research and New Ways of Publications. Springer, New York (2018)

An Overview of Platforms
for Reproducible Research
and Augmented Publications

Miguel Colom[1], Bertrand Kerautret[2(✉)], and Adrien Krähenbühl[3]

[1] Centre de mathématiques et de leurs applications, CNRS, ENS Paris-Saclay,
Université Paris-Saclay, 94235 Cachan Cedex, France
[2] LIRIS, Université de Lyon 2, Lyon, France
bertrand.kerautret@univ-lyon2.fr
[3] ICube, UMR 7357, Université de Strasbourg, Strasbourg, France

Abstract. There exist several dissemination repositories, computation platforms, and online tools that might be used to implement Reproducible Research. In this paper, we discuss the strengths and weaknesses, or better, the adequacy of each of them for this purpose. Specifically, we present aspects such as the freely availability of contents for the scientific community, the languages which are accepted, or how the platform solves the problem of dependency to specific library versions. We discuss if articles and codes are peer-reviewed or if they are simply spread through a dissemination platform, and if changes are allowed after publication. The most popular platforms and tools are presented with the perspective to highlight new ways for scientific communication.

1 Introduction

Reproducibility and replicability are common and usual criteria in many fields as biology, economy, psychology or medicine. Although paramount, meeting these criteria is a goal difficult to achieve. In Computer Science, it is easier since, most of the time, it involves applying the same data to the same algorithm. Ten years ago, Donoho *et al.* mentioned the so-called *credibility crisis* and suggested to not only publish computational results but also the complete source code and data [1]. More recently, this crisis was also mentioned in a research survey where more than 70% of researchers affirm that they fail to reproduce the work of another researcher [2]. Moreover, more than half affirm they fail reproduce their own work. This survey was realized in different domains such as biology, physics and, chemistry.

Before the awareness of this problem, the benefit of Reproducible Research (RR) for authors and computational scientists was illustrated with concrete example from *Wavelet* Matlab package. According to Buckheit *et al.* [3], the package was designed to help implement the reproducible research following the guidelines of Claerbout [4], who defines the scholarship in computational science

© Springer Nature Switzerland AG 2019
B. Kerautret et al. (Eds.): RRPR 2018, LNCS 11455, pp. 25–39, 2019.
https://doi.org/10.1007/978-3-030-23987-9_2

not as the scientific publication but as "the complete software development environment and the complete set of instructions which generated the figures". As shown in the following, RR presents an increasing importance for platforms, in the J. Buckheit *et al.* spirit, with the perspective to define a new way of diffusing scholarship contents.

Several definitions of a reproducible result were proposed. In the following, we consider the definitions by Krijthe and Loog [5] and by Rougier and Hinsen [6]. These authors distinguish two main notions, the *reproducibility* and *replicability*. The reproducibility is defined as the success of a same individual in re-generating the same results with the same inputs and following the same protocols. The replicability reflects the possibility to obtain identical results in a different context without taking the same implementation and protocol of the first authors. It can be considered as valuable since it offers the proof that the proposed scholarship is not only specific to particular conditions but can also be extended to other kinds of situations.

Mainly motivated by reproducible and replicable aspects, new platforms are appearing to help researchers to execute, reproduce, experiment, and compare or diffuse research codes and software, often through an online website. In parallel, other initiatives are growing with introduction of new journals focused on original content as softwares associated to research publications, replication experiences, or specialized in the image processing domain. In the following of this paper, we first present an overview of these platforms (Sect. 2) before comparing them through several criteria (Sect. 3). In addition, we will focus on new initiatives like the *Graphics Replicability Stamp Initiative* that was proposed in conjunction to more classic conferences in order to augment publication with reproduction guarantee (Sect. 4).

2   Overview of Reproducible Research Platforms

In this section we present different types of platforms that could be used to implement RR. We refer to them as:

- **Online execution platforms** (Sect. 2.1): an online platform offering an execution service infrastructure.
- **Dissemination platforms** (Sect. 2.2): their goal is to spread articles, source code, data, and make them public, without necessarily being peer-reviewed.
- **Peer-reviewed journals** (Sect. 2.3): similar to the dissemination platforms, but with an Editorial Board that requests opinion of external experts to decide article acceptance.

2.1   Online Execution Platforms

Some very well-known platforms are closely related to RR in there usages, whether they are domain-specific or more generic.

Galaxy. In the case of Biology, the *Galaxy* project [7–9] started in 2005 as a platform for genomics research making available tools which can be used by non-expert users too. *Galaxy* defines a *workflow* as a reusable template containing different algorithms applied to the input data. In order to achieve reproducibility, the system stores the input dataset, the parameters, the tools and algorithms applied to the data within the chain, and the output dataset. Thus, performing the same workflow with the same data ensures that the same results are obtained, given that the version of all the elements remains the same. The platform allows its users to upload their own data and to adjust the parameters before executing an algorithm. *Galaxy* is made of four main elements: (i) the main public *Galaxy* server featuring tool sets and data for genomics analysis, (ii) open source software and API allowing users to install their own *Galaxy* server, (iii) a repository for developers and administrators, and (iv) the whole community contributing to the development.

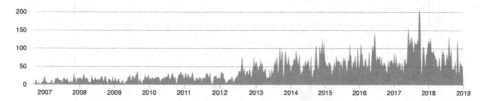

Fig. 1. The *GitHub* activity (in number of commits) of the main *Galaxy* project, extracted from https://github.com/galaxyproject/galaxy.

As shown in Fig. 1, the activity of the *Galaxy* platform is increasing from its beginning and up to now. The *Galaxy* community has a hub[1] that includes yearly conferences (Galaxy Community Conference). This community is also composed of several groups associated to the Intergalactic Utilities Commission, a *Galaxy* training network and an open source package management system. Some regional communities are visible from several countries (Arabic, Austria, France, Japan, UK).

IPython. Generic tools for RR include the *IPython* tool and its notebooks [10]. This mature tool created in 2001 allows to create reproducible articles, not only by editing text in the notebook, but also by allowing code execution and creating figures *in situ*. This approach follows closely the definition of a *reproducible scientific publication* given by Claerbout. Even though the high activity of the platform was during 2011–2015 (from the *GitHub* remote source), this platform is always active and continues to share the main kernel of the *Jupyter* platforms described below.

Jupyter. In 2014 the *Jupyter* project [11] was started as a spin-off of *IPython* in order to separate the *Python* language used in *IPython* from all the other

---

[1] https://galaxyproject.org/community/.

functionalities needed to run the notebooks (for example, the notebook format, the web framework, or the message protocols) [12]. *IPython* turns then into just another computation kernel for *Jupyter*, which nowadays supports more than 40 languages that can be used as kernels[2]. The *Jupyter* notebook also provides new ways to generate interactive webpages from the *nbinteract* viewer [13]. The Fig. 2 illustrates an example of *Jupyter* notebook.

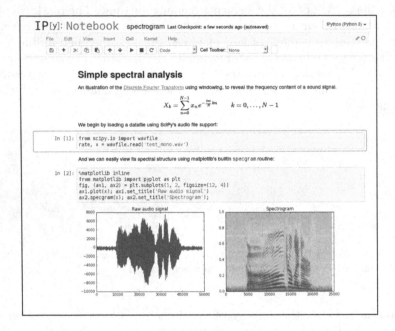

Fig. 2. A *Jupyter* notebook shown online in a web browser.

Jupyter: The Binder Service. Directly related to the *Jupyter* platform, this service offers the possibility to transform any repository containing a *Jupyter* notebook source into an online notebook environment. Therefore, user experiments can be reproduced and executed from a simple *git* repository without installing any *Jupyter* server. The Fig. 3 illustrates the three main steps to reproduce the results of a demonstration code from a git repository. Note that the service is free of charge and no registration is needed to build or run the resulting notebook.

Runmycode.online. In the same line than the previous *Binder* service, this tool is able to execute a source code hosted on an external repository [14]. The website proposes a navigator extension that allows to set the program parameters and start running the code. It can be run online from various code repositories

---

[2] https://github.com/jupyter/jupyter/wiki/Jupyter-kernels.

(a)   (b)   (c)

Fig. 3. The three main steps to build a *Jupyter* online notebook from a git repository: (a) source repository, (b) *Binder* interface, (c) resulting notebook.

as *GitHub*, *GitLab*, or *BitBucket*, and accepts several languages such as C/C++, Java, Nodejs, python. PHP, Ruby, and others. The service is free to use.

Code Ocean. Started in February 2017, this platform [15] is a recent initiative from the IEEE with the aim to attach online demonstrations to the published articles. It defines itself as a *cloud-based computational reproducibility platform*[3]. The platform is only designed to run code and not to really publish article even if a DOI is assigned to each source code. Numerous languages are accepted (Python, R, Julia, Matlab, Octave, C++, Fortran, Perl, Java, Sata, Lua, Octave). There are fees to pay according to the computational load of the servers running the algorithms. A free plan exists, but limited to two concurrent users and 1h/month of computing time.

Note that recently, three Nature journals have run a trial partnership with this platform, allowing authors to demonstrate the reproducibility of their works [16]. Such an initiative could be an interesting answer to the reproducibility crisis mentioned in introduction.

The Fig. 4 illustrates the *Code Ocean* platform that can be executed online. The main view of the platform is composed of sub-views showing the inputs and the results. Note that the source code can also be edited by the user, in a private environment.

The DAE Platform. In the field of document image analysis, the Document Analysis and Exploitation platform (*DAE*) was designed to share and distribute document image with algorithms. Created in 2012, the *DAE* platform contains tools to exploit document annotations and to perform benchmark [17]. Similarly to the previous platforms, *DAE* allows the users to upload their own data and to combine several algorithms. The user can tune the parameters of each of the algorithms proposed by the platform. The users have control over the data uploaded, the parameters used, and the choice of the platform on which the algorithms are available. The Fig. 5 illustrates an example of the *DAE* data sets with different scanned documents. The code is executed exclusively online but is

---

[3] https://codeocean.com.

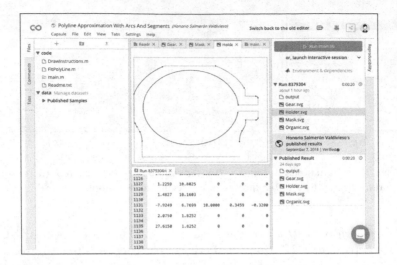

Fig. 4. Development environment of the *Code Ocean* platform, from https://codeocean.com/2018/09/07/polyline-approximation-with-arcs-and-segments

free to use and without any computing time limitation (contrary to *Code Ocean*). The source code of the platform is also open source and available online[4].

The IPOL Journal. It is a full peer-reviewed indexed journal where each paper is associated to an online demonstration and an archive of experiments. The set of online demonstrations [18] can be seen as an online execution platform that share some of the characteristics with *Jupyter*. In particular, *IPOL* proposes to run algorithms online through a web interface, to obtain an immediate visualization of the results and to write algorithms in several programming languages. Moreover, it is free of any cost for authors and users.

IPOL is however exclusively designed to run the demonstration of already published papers. An original point is the fact that it contains the history of the different executions with original source images and parameters. The online demonstrations are build from a simple demo description language avoiding the author to code the demonstration interface himself.

Regarding the system architecture, *IPOL* is built as a Service-Oriented Architecture (SOA) made of micro-services. This type of architecture allows to have simple units (called *modules* in its own terminology, or micro-services) which encapsulate isolated high-level functions. Other examples of service-oriented architectures made of micro-services are *Amazon* AWS API Gateway[5], *Netflix* [19] or *Spotify* [20].

IPOL and *Code Ocean* share many features, as a user-friendly demonstration builder, an online code execution, and an advanced visualization. But they also have some differences since *IPOL* stores all experiments performed by the users

---

[4] https://sourceforge.net/projects/daeplatform.
[5] https://aws.amazon.com/api-gateway.

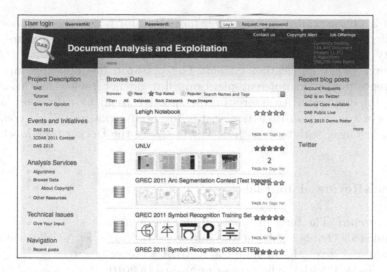

Fig. 5. Example of database available on the *DAE* platform, at address http://dae. cse.lehigh.edu/DAE/?q=browse

in a freely available archive, has demonstrations always free to use, and doesn't require authentication to execute a demonstration.

2.2 Dissemination Platforms

Other generic tools can be seen as *dissemination* platforms since their objective is to make source code and data widely available to everyone. This category contains among others:

- *ResearchCompendia* [21], that stores data and code in an *accessible, traceable, and persistent* form.
- *MLOSS* [22], dedicated to machine learning.
- *DataHub* [23], that allows to create, register, and share generic datasets.
- *RunMyCode* [24], that associates code and data to scientific publications.
- *IPOL*, that, in addition to propose an online execution environment (see Sect. 2.1), makes available the source code of the algorithm.

The various community code development platforms like *GitHub*, *GitLab*, *BitBucket* can also be considered as dissemination platforms since they contribute to diffuse source codes. However, the evolution of the repositories over time is a key question and no guarantees are given from their owners. Despite this, each user can easily replicate a repository to another platform, thanks to the distributed version-control systems, as git or mercurial, on which they are based.

A more global answer to this problem was given in France, leading by the National Institute in Computer Science and Automation (INRIA), at the origin of a project called *Software Heritage*. Its aim is to collect repositories from different platforms into one single place with the plan to ensure their durability [25]. This system is linked to HAL Open Archives System [26], an open source paper publication system. The platform de-duplicates any submitted repository from different platforms but do not review any code nor evaluate the execution. An interesting perspective could be to propose a way to obtain a compilation/execution status for each repository. This could be done, for instance, with tools such as Travis [27] or the Docker framework [28].

2.3   Peer-Reviewed Journals

IPOL Journal. The Image Processing OnLine journal was founded in October 2009 at the initiative of Nicolas Limare and Jean-Michel Morel at CMLA (Université Paris-Saclay), with the first paper published in 2010.
Motivated by RR and first focused on image processing, it differs from classic journals since all articles are provided with (i) a mathematical description of the method, as detailed as possible, (ii) the source code of the presented algorithms, and (iii) an online demonstration [29]. Each demonstration has an archive that stores the history of all executions performed with data from the users. As in classic journals, it has an Editorial Board and every article is assigned an editor that will put the paper under peer-review (both the article and the source code). A mandatory requirement is that each description (pseudo-codes, formulas) given in the text need to match exactly to the source code implementation.

IPOL is an Open Science journal, with an ISSN and a DOI, that contains more than 140 papers covering various image processing subdomains like image de-noising, stereovision, segmentation, 3D mesh processing, or computer graphics. The journal was extended to video and audio processing, as well to general signal processing, including physiological signals.

The main goal is to establish a complete state of the art in algorithms for general signal processing.

ReScienceJournal. This peer-reviewed journal was created in 2015 at the initiative of Konrad Hinsen and Nicolas Rougier. Their motivation follows the replication main goals, as defined by [30] or [5]. *ReScience* aims to promote
already published work and highlights the reproduction of research results in new or different contexts. The authors of the original work are not allowed to submit their own work, even if they claim to have changed their results, architectures, or frameworks. The submission process takes place from the *GitHub* platform with a direct non-anonymous interaction through a *Pull Request* process, used by authors to integrate the new contribution in a shared project. *ReScience* is an online Open Science journal, with article in PDF form. It has a classic organization with volume number, DOI, and reviews available online on *GitHub*.

A typical contribution to *ReScience* is the case of an author who would like reproduce an existing method for which its authors do not propose any implementation. The author can then replicate the method from the original paper and submit his implementation to *ReScience*, including a description of the main steps to reproduce the results.

The journal contains currently 22 accepted contributions, all of them successful replications. Failing replication experiences can also be potentially accepted for publication, even if so far all published papers concern successful replications. A call for replication is diffused on the *GitHub* repository, allowing to suggest the replication of published papers [31]. The call is materialized by adding an *issue* on the repository, from which users can discuss and interact. A more detailed presentation of the journal can be found in a recent article [6].

JOSS Journal. The Journal of Open Source Software was founded by Arfon Smith in May 2016. The motivation to create this new journal comes from the fact that *"Current publishing and citation do not acknowledge software as a first-class research output"* [32]. To answer this, the journal acknowledges  research software and contributes to offer modern computational research results. *JOSS* is a free Open Science journal and similarly to the *ReScience* journal, it is hosted on *GitHub* with a public peer reviewing process that provides direct visibility. As other classic journals it has an ISSN number and the articles a Crossref DOI.

Associated to its source code archive, a *JOSS* publication contains also a *PDF* with a short abstract and a short description of the content with a link to the forked repository of the software. The very short description is voluntary since novel research descriptions is not requested (and not allowed) and is not what the journal is focused on. Publications of APIs are neither allowed. The source code needs to be open source and the submitter needs to be main contributor. Another requirement of the journal is to submit a complete and fully functional product.

The journal covers several domains including Astronomy, Bioinformatics, Computational Science, Data Science, General Engineering, among others. It contains currently more than 551 accepted papers. With a basis of 100 papers per year, the editor of the journal estimates the cost around of $6/paper [32]. The current editor strategy is to handle software versions throughout the publication steps. Requesting major new features can be important to maintain the value for the publications itself while minor updates are also welcome to ensure the maintenance of the software.

Insight J Journal. As JOSS, *Insight J* is an online Open Science journal and covers the domain of medical image processing and visualization [33]. It was created in 2005 by the *Insight Software Consortium* and contains currently 642 publications with 768 peer open reviews. All the publications  do not necessary receive reviews and numerous papers are visible online and do not have any reviews even ten years after publication.

A star based rating process is proposed for any user and allows to evaluate the paper, source code and the review quality. A top ranked list of publications is available along with the number of downloads and views.

Contrary to the *JOSS* journal, *Insight J* is mainly related to a specific library (ITK) and can be seen as a way to increase the value of contributions to this library. Accepted publications usually propose a new module that can be potentially integrated within the library. It generally contains a scientific description with a detailed description of the implementation proposed, using the ITK framework together. The journal has an ISSN number and all its papers are indexed by *Google Scholar*, thus allowing to compute a citation score. The number of citations of the most downloaded paper is relatively low compared to other similar journals. For instance, the *Insight J* paper of Tustison *et al.* [34] was cited 68 times while, for instance, the popular *IPOL* paper of Grompone et al. [35] accounts 373 references. However, it appears that the publications in *Insight J* contribute to promote other associated papers that are published in more general classic journals. For example, an associated paper published in a medical imaging journal [36] obtained 1230 citations.

Notes that two other variants exist with the same form and identical publication process but focused on scientific visualization: the VTK Journal [37] (using VTK library) and the MIDAS journal for visualization and image processing [38].

In the context of RR, these almost new journals offer new complementary alternatives of publication that can break with the usual procedures of scientific communication. The model of the *IPOL* journal follows a larger content model, including scientific descriptions, online demonstrations and perfect matching between algorithms and source codes. More focused on the replication, *ReScience* covers a larger domain and publication related to already known results can foster the discussion in the scientific community. Research software can also be published in the *JOSS* journal whereas contributions on image processing libraries can be proposed to *Insight J*.

3   Comparison

This section summarizes and confronts the characteristics of the previously presented platforms. It shows their strengths and weaknesses as well as opportunities and eventual threats of used approaches. The following criteria are evaluated:

(1) Free to use
(2) No mandatory registration
(3) Several programming languages allowed
(4) Peer-reviewed code and data
(5) Easy to use by the non-expert
(6) General scope
(7) Possibility to upload user data
(8) Interaction through a web interface
(9) Access to a public and persistent archive of experiments
(10) Design of automatic demonstration from textual description or visual tool
(11) Allow to modify the source code before execution

Platform	(1)	(2)	(3)	(4)	(5)	(6)	(7)	(8)	(9)	(10)	(11)
Galaxy	✓	✗	(A)	✓	(B)	✗	✓	✓	✗	✗	✗
DAE	✓	✗	(A)	✓	✗	✗	✓	✓	✗	✗	✗
IPython	✓	✓	✗	–	✗	✓	✗	✗	–	✗	✓
Jupyter	✓	✓	✓	✗	✗	✓	✓	✓	✗	✗	✓
Code Ocean	(C)	✗	✓	✗	(D)	✓	✓	✓	✗	✓	✓
Res. Comp.	✓	✓	✓	✗	✗	✓	✗	✗	✗	–	–
DataHub	✓	✗	–	✗	✓	–	✓	(E)	–	–	–
RunMyCode	✓	✓	✓	✗	✗	✓	✗	(E)	✗	–	–
IPOL	(F)	(G)	✓	✓	✓	✓	✓	✓	✓	✓	✗

Legend	
–	Not Applicable
(A)	It allows users to execute the proposed algorithms, but it is not a dissemination platform and thus it does not accept a list of languages. Instead, it wraps the algorithms and incorporates them
(B)	It frees the user from using command line tools, but it still requires to know the details of the algorithms to perform genomics analysis
(C)	A free plan is offered, but limited to 1h/month of computing time, and a single researcher user. With a cost of $20/month, it allows 10h/month and 5 concurrent users
(D)	A web interface is proposed, but the usability depends on the author who creates its own interface
(E)	The user interacts through a web interface without interactive demonstration
(F)	The demonstrations are free to use up to some limits (say, size of the data or computation time), but industrial use of demonstrations and applications requires payment
(G)	True for demonstrations using a sample learning dataset. To use the platform as a service, the user needs to be connected with a role authorizing this usage

This comparison of platforms should not be seen as a competition to decide if a platform is *better* or *worse* than the others, but as a way to decide which platforms are more adapted to a particular application.

Almost all platforms are free to use (1) with the exception of *Code Ocean*, which offers a very limited free plan.

The possibility of using a platform without a prior registration (2) greatly helps its diffusion and, in the case of scientific applications, it allows spreading knowledge. Some of platforms are mainly oriented to specialists, as for instance *Galaxy* (genomics research).

For any of the platforms publishing source code it is important that at least the most popular languages and frameworks are supported (3). In the case of the *Galaxy* and *DAE* platforms that do not publish algorithms but use them to offer a service, they solve the problem by wrapping the algorithms. In the case of platforms publishing algorithms like *Code Ocean*, *ResearchCompendia*, *RunMyCode*, and *IPOL*, they accept the most popular languages, frameworks and libraries.

About the peer-review of the code (4), *Galaxy* and *DAE* do it before wrapping and incorporating them into their platform, once the interest and opportunity of making publicly available a particular algorithm is clear. Others like *Code Ocean*, *DataHub*, *RunMyCode*, *IPython* and *Jupyter* do not peer-review the code or the data. The code is carefully peer-reviewed only when the platform publishes paper in a journal, like *IPOL*, or when algorithms are offered as a professional service, like *Galaxy* or *DAE*.

In addition to the journal aspect, *IPOL* can be used as a computational platform. It allows users to create *workshops*, which are demonstrations without associated paper. The workshops are not publications and, therefore, are not peer reviewed. This can allow to use *IPOL* as a computational facility in order to, for instance, monetize services. Some platforms such as *Galaxy* or *DAE* try to hide the technical details as the direct calls of tools from the command line and they offer instead a web interface (8). *Jupyter* and *Code Ocean* also hide the direct interaction with the framework by proposing a web interface acting as a proxy for execution and visualization. *IPOL* solves the problem by a flexible interface that can be adapted to each application.

Some of the platforms are domain specific (6) like *Galaxy* or *DAE*, whereas others are more general. This frees the domain-specific platforms to create different web interfaces depending on the final application but, on the other hand, makes them less flexible.

For online execution platforms willing to reach RR, it is mandatory that they allow users to upload their own data (7). And, indeed, all of them propose this functionality. Another interesting add-on is to have a permanent and public archive of experiments (9). In the case of *Galaxy*, *DAE*, *Jupyter*, *Code Ocean*, they are no publicly accessible. Only *IPOL* has a permanent, public and open archive of experiments.

For the platforms which offer demonstrations, an interesting feature is to modify the source code of the method before running the demo (11). This is only found in *Code Ocean*. Both *Code Ocean* and *IPOL* allow to create new demonstrations (10) just with a simple textual description (*IPOL*) or a visual tool (*Code Ocean*).

4   Augmented Publications

The classic way of communicating scientific publications is more and more augmented with new emerging initiatives based on the reproducibility. In the domain of Geometry Processing, the Graphics Replicability Stamp Initiative (GRSI) was created in order to certify the reproduction of both the results and figures contained in the published paper [39]. This initiative was created at the thirteenth *Symposium on Geometry Processing* where it was proposed to authors of accepted papers to apply to this stamp. Note that it was initially known as the *Reproducibility Stamp* and the new *"Replicability"* term differs from the definition used in this paper and is in fact related to the reproducibility. The initiative was continued and extended through collaborations with journals ACM TOG, IEEE TVCG, Elsevier CAGD and Elsevier C&G. Currently 32 contributions received the stamp after 3 years of activity. The contributions are all hosted on the *GitHub* repository.

More related to the *Pattern Recognition* domain, a similar initiative was proposed with the first workshop on Reproducible Research in Pattern Recognition (RRPR 2016) [40]. This satellite workshop was proposed along the ICPR conference and a reproducible label was given to authors of the main conference after review. The aim of the label is to ensure reproducibility of the paper results, i.e. figures and tables. The labeled contributions are also hosted on *GitHub* from a fork of the authors repository.

5   Conclusion

This paper presented an overview of the main structures contributing to facilitate reproducible works. Starting from the RR platforms that change potentially the way the information is spread, we explored four main journals that achieve to make original contributions that go beyond classic publications. We also described recent initiatives allowing to extend or augment classic publication procedures, in particular by showing reproducible results in the form of online algorithm executions. Reproducible Research is absolutely needed to avoid fraud, to establish the state of the art in all involved disciplines, and to definitively ensure reliable scientific practices. All the presented platforms make a valuable contribution in this direction and, with all other mentioned initiatives, will certainly help to disseminate good science and reliable knowledge.

References

1. Donoho, D.L., Maleki, A., Rahman, I.U., Shahram, M., Stodden, V.: Reproducible research in computational harmonic analysis. Comput. Sci. Eng. **11**, 8–18 (2009)
2. Baker, M.: 1,500 scientists lift the lid on reproducibility. Nature **533**, 452 (2016). https://doi.org/10.1038/533452a
3. Buckheit, J.B., Donoho, D.L.: WaveLab and reproducible research. In: Antoniadis, A., Oppenheim, G. (eds.) Wavelets and Statistics. Lecture Notes in Statistics, vol. 103, pp. 55–81. Springer, New York (1995). https://doi.org/10.1007/978-1-4612-2544-7_5
4. Claerbout, J.F., Karrenbach, M.: Electronic documents give reproducible research a new meaning, pp. 601–604 (2005)
5. Krijthe, J.H., Loog, M.: Reproducible pattern recognition research: the case of optimistic SSL. In: Kerautret, B., Colom, M., Monasse, P. (eds.) RRPR 2016. LNCS, vol. 10214, pp. 48–59. Springer, Cham (2017). https://doi.org/10.1007/978-3-319-56414-2_4

6. Rougier, N.P., Hinsen, K.: ReScience C: a journal for reproducible replications in computational science. In: Kerautret, B., et al. (eds.) RRPR 2018. LNCS, vol. 11455, pp. 150–156. Springer, Cham (2019)
7. Giardine, B., et al.: Galaxy: a platform for interactive large-scale genome analysis. Genome Res. **15**, 1451–1455 (2005)
8. Afgan, E., et al.: The Galaxy platform for accessible, reproducible and collaborative biomedical analyses: 2016 update. Nucleic Acids Res. **44**, W3–W10 (2016)
9. Goecks, J., Nekrutenko, A., Taylor, J.: Galaxy: a comprehensive approach for supporting accessible, reproducible, and transparent computational research in the life sciences. Genome Biol. **11**, 1 (2010)
10. Pérez, F., Granger, B.E.: IPython: a system for interactive scientific computing. Comput. Sci. Eng. **9**, 21–29 (2007)
11. et al., P.: Jupyter Project (2018). http://jupyter.org
12. Kluyver, T., et al.: Jupyter Notebooks? A publishing format for reproducible computational workflows. In: Loizides, F., Scmidt, B. (eds.) Positioning and Power in Academic Publishing: Players, Agents and Agendas, pp. 87–90. IOS Press, Amsterdam (2016)
13. Lau, S., Hug, J.: nbinteract: generate interactive web pages from Jupyter notebooks. Master's thesis, EECS Department, University of California, Berkeley (2018)
14. Gupta, S.: RunMyCode (2017). https://runmycode.online. Accessed Apr 2019
15. Code Ocean (2019). https://codeocean.com/. Accessed May 2019
16. Staniland, M.: Nature research journals trial new tools to enhance code peer review and publication. Nature.com Blogs (2018)
17. Lamiroy, B., Lopresti, D.P.: The DAE platform: a framework for reproducible research in document image analysis. In: Kerautret, B., Colom, M., Monasse, P. (eds.) RRPR 2016. LNCS, vol. 10214, pp. 17–29. Springer, Cham (2017). https://doi.org/10.1007/978-3-319-56414-2_2
18. Arévalo, M., Escobar, C., Monasse, P., Monzón, N., Colom, M.: The IPOL Demo system: a scalable architecture of microservices for reproducible research. In: Kerautret, B., Colom, M., Monasse, P. (eds.) RRPR 2016. LNCS, vol. 10214, pp. 3–16. Springer, Cham (2017). https://doi.org/10.1007/978-3-319-56414-2_1
19. Izrailevky, Y.: Completing the netflix cloud migration (2016). https://media.netflix.com/en/company-blog/completing-the-netflix-cloud-migration. Accessed Apr 2019
20. Goldsmith, K.: Microservices at spotify (2016). https://es.slideshare.net/kevingoldsmith/microservices-at-spotify. Accessed Apr 2019
21. Research Compendia (2019). http://researchcompendia.science/. Accessed Apr 2019
22. MLOSS (2019). http://mloss.org. Accessed Apr 2019
23. Datahub (2019). https://datahub.io/. Accessed Apr 2019
24. RunMyCode (2019). http://www.runmycode.org/. Accessed Apr 2019
25. Cosmo, R.D., Zacchiroli, S.: Software heritage: why and how to preserve software source code. In: iPRES 2017: 14th International Conference on Digital Preservation, Kyoto, Japan (2017). https://www.softwareheritage.org
26. Baruch, P.: Open Access Developments in France: the HAL Open Archives System. Learned Publishing **20**, 267–282 (2007). See also; voir aussi: P. Baruch, La diffusion libre du savoir Accès libre et Archives ouvertes. http://archivesic.ccsd.cnrs.fr/sic_00169330/fr/
27. Travis (2019). https://travis-ci.com. Accessed May 2019

28. Docker (2019). https://www.docker.com/. Accessed May 2019
29. Colom, M., Kerautret, B., Limare, N., Monasse, P., Morel, J.M.: IPOL: a new journal for fully reproducible research; analysis of four years development. In: 2015 7th International Conference on New Technologies, Mobility and Security (NTMS), pp. 1–5. IEEE (2015)
30. Patil, P., Peng, R.D., Leek, J.: A statistical definition for reproducibility and replicability. bioRxiv (2016)
31. *GitHub* Call for replication repository (2016). https://github.com/ReScience/call-for-replication
32. Smith, A.M., et al.: Journal of open source software (JOSS): design and first-year review. PeerJ Comput. Sci. **4**, e147 (2017)
33. *Insight J*: Insight journal (2019). ISNN 2327–770X. http://insight-journal.org
34. Tustison, N., Gee, J.: N4ITK: Nick's N3 ITK implementation for MRI bias field correction. Insight J. **9** (2009)
35. Von Gioi, R.G., Jakubowicz, J., Morel, J.M., Randall, G.: LSD: a fast line segment detector with a false detection control. IEEE Trans. Pattern Anal. Mach. Intell. **32**, 722–732 (2010)
36. Tustison, N.J., et al.: N4ITK: improved N3 bias correction. IEEE Trans. Med. Imaging **29**, 1310 (2010)
37. The VTK Journal (2019). ISSN 2328–3459. https://www.vtkjournal.org
38. The MIDAS Journal (2019). ISSN 2182–95432. https://midasjournal.org
39. Panozzo, D.: Graphics replicability stamp initiative (2016). http://www.replicabilitystamp.org. Accessed Apr 2019
40. Kerautret, B., Colom, M., Monasse, P. (eds.): RRPR 2016. LNCS, vol. 10214. Springer, Cham (2017). https://doi.org/10.1007/978-3-319-56414-2

Reproducible Research Results

A Root-to-Leaf Algorithm Computing the Tree of Shapes of an Image

Pascal Monasse[⊠]

LIGM (UMR 8049), École des Ponts, UPE, Champs-sur-Marne, France
`pascal.monasse@enpc.fr`

Abstract. We propose an algorithm computing the tree of shapes of an image, a unified variation of the component trees, proceeding from the root to the leaf shapes in a recursive fashion. It proceeds differently from existing algorithms that start from leaves, which are regional extrema of intensity, and build the intermediate shapes up to the root, which is the whole image. The advantage of the proposed method is a simpler, clearer, and more concise implementation, together with a more favorable running time on natural images. For integer-valued images, the complexity is proportional to the total variation, which is the memory size of the output tree, which makes the algorithm optimal.

Keywords: Tree of shapes · Component trees · Level sets

1 Introduction

1.1 The Tree of Shapes

Extremal regions of an image are connected regions of an image where the intensity is above or below a certain gray level. These generalize the shapes of the classical mathematical morphology of binary images to gray-scale. Indeed, this just amounts to binarize the gray level image at a certain level and consider the resulting shapes. As there is not a single threshold where interesting shapes occur, all possible thresholds should be applied. For example, for an 8-bit image, all integer values from 0 to 255 can be used as thresholds. It is clear that when the threshold increases, minimal regions (those below the threshold) increase with respect to set inclusion, while maximal regions decrease. From these simple observations, two trees can be built, the minimal and the maximal trees, called the component trees. In each tree, a shape is an ancestor of another if the first contains the second. The root is the full set of pixels, obtained at threshold 255 in the min-tree and 0 in the max-tree. These observations are at the basis of efficient algorithms to compute the component trees, either bottom-up, i.e., from the leaves to the root [2,20], or top-down, from the root to the leaves [21,22]. While some of these algorithms are very efficient for 8-bit images, others beat the former on higher bit depths. A full comparison is available in the literature [4].

© Springer Nature Switzerland AG 2019
B. Kerautret et al. (Eds.): RRPR 2018, LNCS 11455, pp. 43–54, 2019.
https://doi.org/10.1007/978-3-030-23987-9_3

Naturally, not all extremal regions are significant or are the projection of a single 3D object in the image. However, a simple criterion, like a high contrast, can be enough to recover some important shapes that may be used as features in image registration or disparity estimation. This is the principle at the basis of maximally stable extremal regions (MSER) [14], which yield point correspondences between images of the same scene in the same manner as the similarity invariant feature transform (SIFT) [13] and its variants. A more recent alternative to MSER is shapes just before their merging in a component tree, so-called tree-based Morse regions [26]. Some of these methods are compared in a famous study [16].

The need for extraction of both component trees can be lifted by using the tree of shapes [18]. The shapes involved in this construction are built from the connected components of extremal regions. The internal holes of the latter, that is all bounded connected components of their complement except one, the exterior, are filled, yielding the shapes. It happens that shapes, whether issued from minimal or maximal extremal regions, can still be ordered in an inclusion tree [1]. This unique structure is well suited for contrast-invariant filtering [6,19], self-dual filtering [10,12], segmentation [24,25], or image registration [9,17].

1.2 Related Work

The computation of the tree of shapes can be done by merging the component trees [5]. The advantage is that the algorithm works in any dimension, but it is not particularly efficient for 2D images. The standard algorithm, the fast level set transform (FLST) [7], works in a bottom-up fashion, starting from the leaves and leveling the image after each extraction of shape [15]. Interpreting the image as a continuous bilinear interpolated surface yields the tree of bilinear level lines, which can be efficiently computed based on level lines [7,8], which is akin to the proposed algorithm. The closer to the proposed algorithm is top-down [23], from root to leaves, but only applicable to hexagonal connectivity, while ours works in the standard 4- and 8-connectivity. Finally, a different definition of shapes based on multi-valued images [11] has the potential to be computed very efficiently, but no public implementation seems available.

1.3 Background and Notations

We consider discrete images I defined on pixels. Each pixel $p \in \{0, \ldots, w-1\} \times \{0, \ldots, h-1\}$ gets a value $I(p) \in \mathbb{R}$. We consider the extremal regions, or level sets: $\{p : I(p) \leq \lambda\}$ and $\{p : I(p) \geq \lambda\}$. The 4-connected components of the former are called inferior components and the 8-connected components of the latter are called superior components. The asymmetry is necessary here to get an inclusion tree later on. Assuming a component C not touching the image boundary $\{0, w-1\} \times \{0, \ldots, h-1\} \cup \{0, \ldots, w-1\} \times \{0, h-1\}$, we can fill all connected components of its complement (8-connected if C is an inferior component, 4-connected otherwise) except the one containing the image boundary, yielding a shape S. The shapes built from all such components, together with the set of all pixels R, has an inclusion tree structure: A shape S is an ancestor of another S' iff $S' \subset S$. If S and S' are not nested like here, then $S \cap S' = \emptyset$. Since any pixel p is inside a shape (at least R), we can consider all shapes containing p, which are nested since they intersect; the smallest of them is noted $S[p]$. Pixels $p_1, \ldots, p_k$ such that $S = S[p_1] = \cdots = S[p_k]$ are called the private pixels of S. In that case, we must have $I[p_1] = \cdots = I[p_k]$, called the gray level g of S. A pixel p in S having a 4-neighbor (if S is inferior) or 8-neighbor (if S is superior) q outside S is said to be at the boundary of S, while q is said to be an external neighbor of S. It seems that all private pixels of S are at its boundary or connected to such a pixel inside the iso-level $I_g := \{p : I(p) = g\}$. Actually, this is not all, since all pixels at the external boundary of a *child* shape of S in the tree having gray level g and their connected components in I_g are also private pixels. This is illustrated Fig. 1. The private pixels of shape B are two components of iso-level at the boundary, together with another component *not* at the boundary, but at the immediate exterior of C and D, children of B.

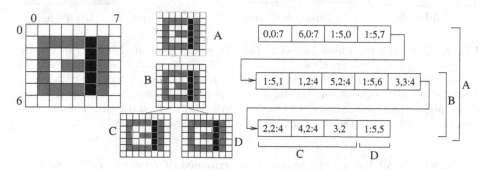

Fig. 1. Tree of shapes of a 7×8 image. The boundaries (level lines) of superior shapes are in red and of inferior shapes in blue. The root is A, its child is B, whose children are C and D. On the right, the arrangement of pixels according to their smallest shape (Matlab range notation).

2   Following a Level Line

The key element of the algorithm is that it is based on level lines rather than level sets. A shape is the "interior region" delimited by a level line and the level line is the boundary of the shape. Each level line is trodden twice by the algorithm: the first time to extract the level line itself and find the gray level of the shape, along with one private pixel; the second time to find possible additional private pixels of the parent shape that are not connected to its boundary.

The level line is a sequence of consecutive edgels. An edgel ("edge element") can be represented as the common boundary between two adjacent pixels, that is pixels for which one or two coordinates, x and y, differ by one unit. In order to ensure that each pixel is involved in exactly 8 edgels and to avoid exceptions for pixels at the boundary of the image, we represent rather an edgel by one pixel and one cardinal direction: east (E), north (N), west (W) or south (S), and the diagonal directions. An edgel is thus *oriented*, and the pixel is called its interior pixel, while its exterior pixel, if it exists, is the pixel adjacent to the interior one across the direction, see Fig. 2(a). Consecutive edgels either share a common interior pixel (we say the level line "turns left") or a common exterior pixel (the level line "turns right"), or have their interior pixels adjacent along their identical directions (the level line "goes straight").

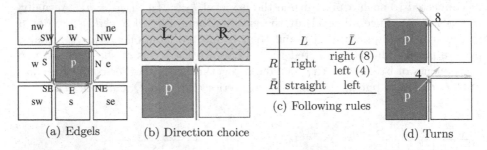

(a) Edgels   (b) Direction choice   (d) Turns

Fig. 2. Edgels and level lines following. (a) The edgels associated to interior pixel p are for example $(p, s) = (p, E)$ and $(p, ne) = (p, NW)$, the latter being diagonal. (b) When following a level line (here at edgel (p, N)), the new edgel depends on whether L and R are within the shape. (c) Rules for next edgel, depending on whether L and R are above the threshold or not ($\bar{L}$ and $\bar{R}$). (d) Turns left and right. The diagonal direction is followed iff the connexity matches the displayed number.

To be a level line of the image I, a sequence of consecutive edgels $L = (e_0, \ldots, e_{n-1}, e_n = e_0)$, with $e_i \neq e_j$ for $0 \leq i < j < n$, must satisfy

$$g := \max_{0 \leq i < n} I(\mathrm{Int}(e_i)) < \min_{0 \leq i < n} I(\mathrm{Ext}(e_i)) \text{ or} \tag{1}$$

$$g := \min_{0 \leq i < n} I(\mathrm{Int}(e_i)) > \max_{0 \leq i < n} I(\mathrm{Ext}(e_i)). \tag{2}$$

In the first case, we say that L is an inferior level line, which is the boundary of an inferior shape, while in the second case L is a superior level line, boundary of a superior shape. In any case, the gray level g is called the level of L and of the shape whose boundary is L. In the above formulas, intensities of nonexistent exterior pixels are replaced by $-\infty$. If no exterior pixel exists in the sequence, that is, L follows the boundary of I, the right-hand side becomes $-\infty$ and we are in the second alternative, a superior level line that is the boundary of the root shape. In general, any edgel with no exterior pixel is of superior type[1]. Their order indicates the type of the level line.

As soon as we have an edgel e with $I(\mathrm{Int}(e)) \neq I(\mathrm{Ext}(e))$, e is in a level line of I. In our algorithm, we need to find the largest shape, in the sense of set

---

[1] This choice is arbitrary, we could have chosen $+\infty$ and the root shape would have been of inferior type.

inclusion, whose boundary L includes e, that is, the one whose gray level g is as close as possible to $I(\text{Ext}(e))$, which may be different from $I(\text{Int}(e))$. Starting from e, we need to find the following one in the sequence $\mathcal{L}(e)$ we are building. We iterate this until we reach again e. For this, the procedure needs to know which direction to follow (left turn, right turn, or straight ahead). This depends on the gray levels of two pixels, L and R in Fig. 2(b). The rules for finding the next edgel are in Fig. 2(c) according to whether L (resp. R) is in the shape or not, the latter case being noted $\bar{L}$ (resp. $\bar{R}$). The rule indicates which direction to take: straight means continue to the direction of the arrow, that is, the interior pixel becomes L and the direction does not change. The indications "left" and "right" indicate a turning direction. In a left turn, the interior pixel remains the same, but not in a right turn. The complex case is $\bar{L} \wedge R$, which is a saddle point. The turn to take depends on the connexity: left for 4-connexity and right for 8-connexity. Performing a turn is explained by Fig. 2(d). A left turn is performed in two steps in 8-connexity, first with a diagonal direction (current direction N would be followed by NW, then W in the illustration), and also for a right turn in 4-connexity (NE then E). The procedure to follow a level line is summarized in Algorithm 1. According to Fig. 2(d), left and right turns can actually generate two edgels depending on connexity. In such case, the first edgel appended is diagonal, and the following edgel finishes the turn.

Data: Edgel e_0, with $I(\text{Int}(e_0)) \neq I(\text{Ext}(e_0))$
Result: $\mathcal{L}(e_0) = (e_0, \ldots, e_{n-1}, e_n = e_0)$: largest level line through e_0
$\lambda \leftarrow I(\text{Ext}(e_0))$
repeat
$\quad$ $l \leftarrow \text{Int}(\textbf{go\_straight}(e_i))$, $r \leftarrow \text{Ext}(\textbf{go\_straight}(e_i))$
$\quad$ $L \leftarrow \text{sign}(I(l) - \lambda) = \text{sign}(I(\text{Int}(e_0)) - \lambda)$
$\quad$ $R \leftarrow \text{sign}(I(r) - \lambda) = \text{sign}(I(\text{Int}(e_0)) - \lambda)$
$\quad$ **if** $L \wedge R$ **then** $e_{i+1} \leftarrow \textbf{turn\_right}(e_i)$
$\quad$ **if** $L \wedge \bar{R}$ **then** $e_{i+1} \leftarrow \textbf{go\_straight}(e_i)$
$\quad$ **if** $\bar{L} \wedge \bar{R}$ **then** $e_{i+1} \leftarrow \textbf{turn\_left}(e_i)$
$\quad$ **if** $\bar{L} \wedge R$ **then** $\quad\quad\quad$ // Saddle point: turn depending on connexity
$\quad\quad$ **if** $I(\text{Int}(e_0)) > \lambda$ **then** $e_{i+1} \leftarrow \textbf{turn\_right}(e_i)$
$\quad\quad$ **else** $e_{i+1} \leftarrow \textbf{turn\_left}(e_i)$
$\quad$ $i \leftarrow i + 1$
until $e_i = e_0$

Algorithm 1. Follow a level line from an initial edgel

3 Top-Down Algorithm

3.1 Representation of the Tree

A shape is stored as a structure comprising its type (inferior or superior), its level g, its contour (array of positions) and an array of its pixels. Moreover, it contains pointers to its parent shape, its "first" child, and its next sibling, if any. In that manner, all children of a shape form a list structure. This is all that is required for walking the tree in any way. Pixels are stored taking advantage of nesting: private pixels of a shape come first in the array, followed by arrays of pixels of its children. This recursive ordering allows to have a single array containing a permutation of all pixels of the image, and each shape has a pointer for its beginning and a pointer to its end inside this array (see Fig. 1). Notice also that such an arrangement provides an $O(1)$ procedure to determine whether one shape is a descendant of another, by comparison of pointers.

The tree is represented as an array of shapes[2]. It stores also an index S[p], giving for each pixel p the shape of which it is a private pixel.

3.2 Top-Down Recursive Extraction

The algorithm 2 starts from an edgel e whose internal and external pixels have different intensities. The procedure create_tree builds the shape S whose boundary is $\mathcal{L}(e)$, and recursively the tree rooted at S. In order to do that, the first loop of the algorithm follows $\mathcal{L}(e)$ and stores a single internal pixel p, which is a private pixel of S. Its gray level g is the closest to $I(\text{Ext}(e))$ among all internal pixels of edges in $\mathcal{L}(e)$. This loop also reinitializes $S[.]$ to $\emptyset$ at each interior pixel. This is necessary since the call of find_pp_children from the parent P (procedure detailed below) has overwritten it with tag P. After this loop, the level g of S is stored and the registered private pixel p is put into a queue Q. The tag $S[p]$ is set to S, like all subsequent pixels pushed into Q.

Data: edgel e
Result: Tree rooted at largest shape S whose level line L goes through e
$\lambda \leftarrow I(\text{Ext}(e))$ // Level of parent
$p \leftarrow \text{Int}(e)$
for $e_i \in \mathcal{L}(e)$ **do**   // Line following, Algorithm 1
     $S[\text{Int}(e_i)] \leftarrow \emptyset$
     if $|I(\text{Int}(e_i)) - \lambda| < |I(p) - \lambda|$ **then**
         $p \leftarrow \text{Int}(e_i)$
$S.\text{type} \leftarrow \begin{cases} \inf & \text{if } I(p) < \lambda \\ \sup & \text{if } I(p) > \lambda \end{cases}$
$S.g \leftarrow I(p), S[p] \leftarrow S$
$C \leftarrow \text{find\_pp\_children}(S, p)$ // C is an array of edgels
for $e_i \in C$ **do**
     $S' \leftarrow \text{create\_tree}(e_i)$ // Recursive call for children
     Insert S' as child of S

Algorithm 2. create_tree, main routine

---

[2] The first shape in the array is the root, corresponding to the full image, and parents have a position before their children. This is a consequence of the top-down nature of the algorithm.

All pixels that will transit in Q will be the private pixels of S. The second step (Algorithm 3) dequeues the waiting pixel p from Q and examines its neighbors (4- or 8-neighbors depending on the type of S). For each one q not already explored ($S[p] = \emptyset$), we have two possibilities: if $I[p] = I[q]$, q is also a private pixel, it is marked as explored ($S[q] = S$) and inserted in Q. Otherwise, the edgel $e = (q, p)$ is on a level line $\mathcal{L}(e)$ bounding a shape that is a child of S. This edgel is put in an array C for later treatment. The level line $\mathcal{L}(e)$ is followed, with a twofold goal: mark internal pixels r as explored ($S[r] = S$) so as to prevent a re-exploration from a different edgel; if an exterior pixel r is unmarked and $I(p) = g$, mark r and enqueue it in Q, since it is a private pixel.

Data: Shape S, one private pixel p_0
Result: Find *all* private pixels of S; Return array C of edgels, one per child
             level line.

$Q \leftarrow p_0$ `// Push p₀ in a queue`
while $Q \neq \emptyset$ **do**
    $Q \rightarrow p$ `// Pop pixel from Q, store in p`
    Add p as private pixel of S
    for $q \sim p$ **and** $S[q] = \emptyset$ **do**   `// Unexplored neighbors of p`
       $S[q] \leftarrow S$
       if $I(q) = I(p)$ **then**
          $Q \leftarrow q$ `// Push q, private pixel`
       else
          $e = (q, p)$ `// Edgel with q as interior pixel`
          $C \leftarrow e$
          for $e_i \in \mathcal{L}(e)$ **do**
             $S[\mathrm{Int}(e_i)] \leftarrow S$
             if $S[\mathrm{Ext}(e_i)] = \emptyset$ **and** $I(\mathrm{Ext}(e_i)) = S.g$ **then**
               $Q \leftarrow \mathrm{Ext}(e_i)$ `// This is a private pixel`
               $S[\mathrm{Ext}(e_i)] \leftarrow S$

Algorithm 3. `find_pp_children`, find private pixels of S and one edge per child level line

---

Each edgel in C is at the boundary of a different child of S. At this point, all internal and all external pixels of an edgel along the boundary of S is marked by $S[p] = S$. Each one provokes a recursive call to `create_tree`, whose first step puts back internal pixels along the boundary to $\emptyset$, as seen above.

3.3 Complexity

At any edgel e, there are at most $|I(\mathrm{Int}(e)) - I(\mathrm{Ext}(e))|$ level lines going through e if I takes only integer values. Each level line is followed twice, so that the complexity of the algorithm is

$$O(\sum_{p \sim p'} |I(p) - I(p')|) = O(\mathrm{TV}(I)), \tag{3}$$

the (discrete) total variation of I. Notice that if level lines are stored with the shapes, this complexity is asymptotically optimal, since it is proportional to the output size. However, for large images storing the level lines can be too demanding, and our code makes this storage optional at compile time.

3.4   Comparison with the FLST

The reference algorithm for extraction of the tree of shapes is the FLST [7]. Its high level operation is summarized in Algorithm 4. Its procedure is bottom-up, that is, it starts from leaves and goes up to the root of the tree.

```
 1  for pixel p do
 2      if p local extremum then
 3          while true do
 4              Extract iso-level S = cc({I = I(p)}, p)
 5              if S regional extremum without hole then
 6                  Insert S as new shape in tree
 7                  for q ∈ S do
 8                      if S[q] = ∅ then
 9                          S[q] ← S
10                      else
11                          I(q) ← I(p)
12                          Add highest ancestor of S[q] as child of S
13                  p ← neighbor of S of closest intensity to I(p)
14              else
15                  break while loop
```

Algorithm 4. High-level operation of the FLST.

It relies on the observation that a leaf of the tree of shapes is a regional extremum of the image with hole, and that a regional extremum contains a local extremum. Pixels are thus sequentially scanned, and when a local extremum p is met, the procedure tries to extract a shape and its ancestors:

1. The set S of pixels connected to p at the same level $I(p)$ are extracted by region growing;
2. If S is a regional extremum without hole then S is a new shape, all pixels q of S with no smallest associated yet are private pixels of S, while other pixels of S are set to level $I(p)$ and their largest ancestor yet (upper-most parent of $S[q]$ is set as a child of S.
3. p is moved to a neighbor of S of closest intensity to $I(p)$ and we continue to step 1, that is we try going up the tree. It can be noticed that the new S will be a superset of the current one, so the region growing needs not start from the single pixel p.

The bottleneck of the algorithm is the abortion of the `while` loop at line 15, whose goal is to walk up the tree (to the root), when the set S presents one or several internal holes: these holes are filled one by one at line 11, but only the last one is able to proceed up the tree and extract S as a shape.

The worst case scenario for the FLST is in the presence of a large uniform area with many holes, for example a checkerboard. Each black case of one pixel is a hole in the white shape, so that the complexity is $O(n^2)$ with n the number of pixels. By contrast, the proposed algorithm does not have any particular trouble with such a situation, yielding a complexity $O(n)$.

On the contrary, when a deep hierarchy of nested shapes is present, the proposed algorithm is quite slow, since a new level line has to be followed for each one. This worst situation can happen for high bit-depth image, typically when each pixel has its own single gray level. There are as many shapes as pixels, and the length of level lines could be also large. Another trouble is that the recursivity follows the tree depth and could result in a memory stack overflow. In this situation, the FLST has no difficulty at all, just walking up the tree shape by shape without break.

Roughly speaking, the proposed algorithm is advantageous for low bit-depth images and wide (many children) but shallow trees, while the FLST prefers narrow (few children) but deep trees. It happens that for 8-bit images, the former is more frequent than the latter. This is demonstrated by the experiments of the next section.

4   Experiments

Our implementation[3] is coded in C++. The core of the algorithm is about 250 lines of code. It is compiled with the GNU compiler gcc version 4.8 in optimized mode and run on an Intel Xeon CPU E5-2643 at 3.3 GHz. Experiments are performed on different crops of large Wikipedia images. Each crop is at the center of image. Run times of the proposed algorithm and of the classical FLST are in Fig. 3.

On the *Church* image[4], a regular photograph, both the proposed algorithm and the classical FLST are performing well, with a significant advantage for the proposed algorithm beginning at about 10 Mpixels. Notice the time spent for our algorithm is roughly linear, so as the TV. For the *Meteo* image[5], a satellite image, our algorithm is quite fast even at high resolution, while the classical FLST seems to have a super-linear running time. Speed-ups of our algorithm are very significant here. Finally, for a simple *Cartoon* image[6], with a low TV, our algorithm performs very well (5 seconds at 20 Mpixels), while the classical FLST takes above 120 seconds at 5 Mpixels, and more than 500 seconds at 9 Mpixels. This is because such a situation is not favorable to the FLST, with some shapes

---

[3] https://github.com/pmonasse/flst.

[4] https://upload.wikimedia.org/wikipedia/commons/5/5e/12-04-06-senftenhuette-by-RalfR-08.jpg.

[5] https://upload.wikimedia.org/wikipedia/commons/6/6b/02S_Dec_8_2011_0600Z.jpg.

[6] https://upload.wikimedia.org/wikipedia/commons/6/6c/0-cynefin-ORIGINEEL.jpg.

having a high number of children. Each time a child is extracted, the FLST levels it to the gray level of the parent, until it realizes that more children are to be extracted. In such a situation, the path going up the tree has to stop until all children are extracted. The proposed algorithm has no such problem.

The proposed algorithm extracts the tree of shapes of *Church* (60 Mpixels) in 54 s, of *Meteo* (56 Mpixels) in 32 s, and of *Cartoon* (300 Mpixels) in 85 s. This shows that the algorithm, although single thread, is able to handle large images in reasonable time.

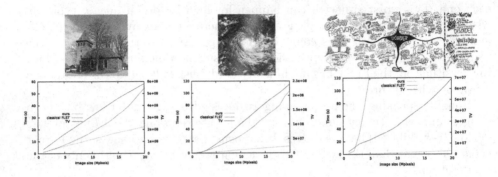

Fig. 3. Run-time with respect to image size.

5   Conclusion

We have presented an algorithm that computes the tree of shapes by starting from the root and proceeding downward to the leaves. Experiments show that it is more efficient on natural images, and the algorithm is even optimal on integer-valued images.

One minor drawback is that the current implementation assumes a priori a fixed gray level outside the image frame, whereas its prime concurrent, the FLST, adapts to the image contents. A possible solution to recover this feature is to compute two trees, one when the outside is below the minimal value in the image and the other where it is above the maximal value. However, the root-to-leaf extraction of the second tree can be stopped as soon as shapes do not meet the image boundary, because these shapes are common to both trees. It remains only to sort the shapes meeting the boundary from both trees to put them in the correct hierarchy [5].

Further experiments would be needed in order to compare with a modified version of the FLST that extracts the full tree in several passes with increasing maximal area [7], which alleviates the problem of wide trees. Another worthwile comparison is with a quasi-linear algorithm that transforms the extraction to a max-tree computation into a larger image [3].

A possible extension of the algorithm is to derive a parallel implementation for handling extra-large images. Indeed, since extracting a subtree rooted at some node of the tree has no side-effect on its exterior, i.e., the rest of the image, different threads could handle the bifurcations in the tree (several children to common parent), each one building the subtree rooted at a sibling, without need for synchronization. This is in strong contrast to bottom-up algorithms where threads building up from different leaves would need to wait for each other when they have to merge at their common ancestor.

References

1. Ballester, C., Caselles, V., Monasse, P.: The tree of shapes of an image. ESAIM: COCV **9**, 1–18 (2003)
2. Berger, C., Géraud, T., Levillain, R., Widynski, N., Baillard, A., Bertin, E.: Effective component tree computation with application to pattern recognition in astronomical imaging. In: IEEE International Conference on Image Processing, 2007, ICIP 2007, vol. 4, pp. IV-41. IEEE (2007)
3. Carlinet, E., Crozet, S., Géraud, T.: The tree of shapes turned into a max-tree: a simple and efficient linear algorithm. In: Proceedings of the IEEE International Conference on Image Processing (ICIP) (2018)
4. Carlinet, E., Géraud, T.: A comparative review of component tree computation algorithms. IEEE Trans. Image Process. **23**(9), 3885–3895 (2014)
5. Caselles, V., Meinhardt, E., Monasse, P.: Constructing the tree of shapes of an image by fusion of the trees of connected components of upper and lower level sets. Positivity **12**(1), 55–73 (2008)
6. Caselles, V., Monasse, P.: Grain filters. J. Math. Imaging Vision **17**(3), 249–270 (2002)
7. Caselles, V., Monasse, P.: Geometric Description of Images as Topographic Maps. Lecture Notes in Computer Science, vol. 1984. Springer, Heidelberg (2009)
8. Ciomaga, A., Monasse, P., Morel, J.M.: The image curvature microscope: accurate curvature computation at subpixel resolution. Image Process. Line **7**, 197–217 (2017). https://doi.org/10.5201/ipol.2017.212
9. Dibos, F., Koepfler, G., Monasse, P.: Image alignment. Geometric Level Set Methods in Imaging, Vision, and Graphics, pp. 271–295. Springer, New York (2003)
10. Dibos, F., Koepfler, G., Monasse, P.: Total Variation Minimization for Scalar/Vector Regularization, pp. 121–140. Springer, New York (2003)
11. Géraud, T., Carlinet, E., Crozet, S., Najman, L.: A quasi-linear algorithm to compute the tree of shapes of nD images. In: Hendriks, C.L.L., Borgefors, G., Strand, R. (eds.) ISMM 2013. LNCS, vol. 7883, pp. 98–110. Springer, Heidelberg (2013). https://doi.org/10.1007/978-3-642-38294-9_9
12. Keshet, R.: Shape-tree semilattice. J. Math. Imaging Vision **22**(2–3), 309–331 (2005)
13. Lowe, D.G.: Object recognition from local scale-invariant features. In: The Proceedings of the Seventh IEEE International Conference on Computer Vision, 1999, vol. 2, pp. 1150–1157. IEEE (1999)
14. Matas, J., Chum, O., Urban, M., Pajdla, T.: Robust wide-baseline stereo from maximally stable extremal regions. Image Vision Comput. **22**(10), 761–767 (2004)
15. Meyer, F., Maragos, P.: Nonlinear scale-space representation with morphological levelings. J. Vis. Commun. Image Represent. **11**(2), 245–265 (2000)
16. Mikolajczyk, K., Schmid, C.: A performance evaluation of local descriptors. IEEE Trans. Pattern Anal. Mach. Intell. **27**(10), 1615–1630 (2005)

17. Monasse, P.: Contrast invariant registration of images. In: 1999 IEEE International Conference on Acoustics, Speech, and Signal Processing, 1999. Proceedings, vol. 6, pp. 3221–3224. IEEE (1999)
18. Monasse, P., Guichard, F.: Fast computation of a contrast-invariant image representation. IEEE Trans. Image Process. **9**(5), 860–872 (2000)
19. Monasse, P., Guichard, F.: Scale-space from a level lines tree. J. Vis. Commun. Image Represent. **11**(2), 224–236 (2000)
20. Najman, L., Couprie, M.: Building the component tree in quasi-linear time. IEEE Trans. Image Process. **15**(11), 3531–3539 (2006)
21. Nistér, D., Stewénius, H.: Linear time maximally stable extremal regions. In: Forsyth, D., Torr, P., Zisserman, A. (eds.) ECCV 2008. LNCS, vol. 5303, pp. 183–196. Springer, Heidelberg (2008). https://doi.org/10.1007/978-3-540-88688-4_14
22. Salembier, P., Oliveras, A., Garrido, L.: Antiextensive connected operators for image and sequence processing. IEEE Trans. Image Process. **7**(4), 555–570 (1998)
23. Song, Y.: A topdown algorithm for computation of level line trees. IEEE Trans. Image Process. **16**(8), 2107–2116 (2007)
24. Xu, Y., Carlinet, E., Géraud, T., Najman, L.: Hierarchical segmentation using tree-based shape spaces. IEEE Trans. Pattern Anal. Mach. Intell. **39**(3), 457–469 (2017)
25. Xu, Y., Géraud, T., Najman, L.: Context-based energy estimator: application to object segmentation on the tree of shapes. In: 2012 19th IEEE International Conference on Image Processing (ICIP), pp. 1577–1580. IEEE (2012)
26. Xu, Y., Monasse, P., Géraud, T., Najman, L.: Tree-based morse regions: a topological approach to local feature detection. IEEE Trans. Image Process. **23**(12), 5612–5625 (2014)

Discrete Regular Polygons for Digital Shape Rigid Motion via Polygonization

Phuc Ngo[1,2(✉)], Yukiko Kenmochi[3], Nicolas Passat[4],
and Isabelle Debled-Rennesson[1,2]

[1] Université de Lorraine, LORIA, UMR 7503,
54506 Vandoeuvre-lès-Nancy, France
{hoai-diem-phuc.ngo,isabelle.debled-rennesson}@loria.fr
[2] CNRS, LORIA, UMR 7503, 54506 Vandoeuvre-lès-Nancy, France
[3] Université Paris-Est, LIGM, CNRS, Paris, France
yukiko.kenmochi@esiee.fr
[4] Université de Reims Champagne-Ardenne, CReSTIC, Reims, France
nicolas.passat@univ-reims.fr

Abstract. Recently, a sufficient condition, namely *quasi-regularity*, has been proposed for preserving the connectivity during the process of digitization of a continuous object whose boundary is not necessarily differentiable. Under this condition, a rigid motion scheme for digital objects of $\mathbb{Z}^2$ is proposed to guarantee that a well-composed object will remain well-composed, and its global geometry will be approximately preserved. In this paper, we are interested in polygons generated from digital objects and their rigid motions in $\mathbb{Z}^2$. For this, we introduce a notion of *discrete regularity* which is a restriction of quasi-regularity for polygons. This notion provides a simple geometric verification, based on the measure of lengths and angles, of quasi-regularity which is originally defined with morphological operators. Furthermore, we present a method for geometry-preserving rigid motions based on convex decomposition of polygons. This paper focuses on, the implementation and on the reproduction of the method linking to an online demonstration. The way of using the C++ source code in other contexts is shown as well.

Keywords: Rigid motion · Digital topology · Quasi-regularity ·
Well-composedness

1 Introduction

Rigid motions (*i.e.* transformations based on translations and rotations) are involved in many image processing and analysis applications (*e.g.* segmentation [2], classification [1], registration [24] or tracking [23]). In such applications, the input data are usually digital images which are obtained by sampling and quantification, namely a *digitization*, of continuous objects. Due to the digitization, the resulting digital object may have different properties than those of the original continuous one [6].

© Springer Nature Switzerland AG 2019
B. Kerautret et al. (Eds.): RRPR 2018, LNCS 11455, pp. 55–70, 2019.
https://doi.org/10.1007/978-3-030-23987-9_4

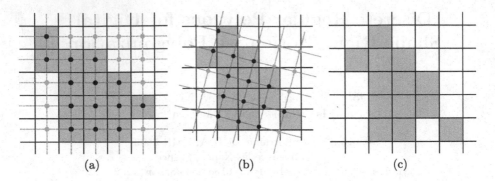

Fig. 1. (a) $\mathsf{X} \subset \mathbb{Z}^2$ with the square grid of $\mathbb{Z}^2$ and the associated Voronoi cell boundaries. (b) Rigid motion followed by a digitization applied on the square grid of (a). (c) The transformed result which is not topologically equivalent to (a); the object is split into two components if we consider the 4-connectivity.

In this article, we are interested in rigid motions on digital images defined on $\mathbb{Z}^2$. Contrary to rigid motions in $\mathbb{R}^2$ which are well-known as topology- and geometry-preserving operations, the rigid motions defined on $\mathbb{Z}^2$ generally do not preserve these properties, as illustrated in Fig. 1. In this context, some studies were recently proposed for providing topological guarantees when applying rigid motions on digital objects [15,16]. Besides, a method is proposed in [13] for convexity and connectivity-preserving rigid motions on $\mathbb{Z}^2$.

In [14], a morphology-based notion, called *quasi-r-regularity*, has been presented together with a rigid motion model that allows to preserve topology and geometry of the shape of the digital object, in particular those of its boundary, under arbitrary rigid motions. Inspired by this work, we investigate this notion in a discrete geometrical way for polygonal objects. More precisely, we introduce the notion of *discrete-r-regularity* which is a restricted *quasi-r-regularity* to polygons. Furthermore, we propose an implementation of the rigid motion scheme based on polygonal modelling of digital objects in [16] using a convex decomposition of polygons. More specifically, we use a (continuous) polygon P generated from a digital object X with some conditions such as $\mathsf{X} = \mathrm{P}(\mathsf{X}) \cap \mathbb{Z}^2$; we transform and digitize this polygon for obtaining a final transformed digital object in $\mathbb{Z}^2$. We show that the topology and some geometric properties of X are preserved under rigid motions if the polygon is discrete-1-regular.

This article is organized as follows. In Sect. 2, we recall useful notions. The main results with the method of rigid motion are presented in Sect. 3. Then, we describe the codes and how to reproduce results in Sect. 4.

2   Preliminaries

2.1   Digitization and Topology Preservation

A digital object $\mathsf{X} \subset \mathbb{Z}^2$ is generally obtained as the result of a digitization process applied on a continuous object $\mathsf{X} \subset \mathbb{R}^2$. In this work, we consider the

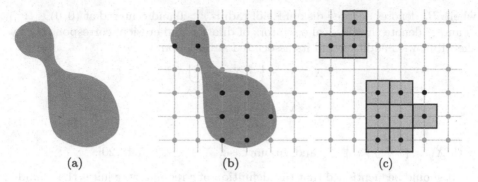

Fig. 2. (a) A continuous object X in $\mathbb{R}^2$. (b) A Gauss digitization of X, leading to the definition of X which is composed by the black points of $\mathbb{Z}^2$ within X. (c) The digital object X represented as a set of pixels. The objects X and X are not topologically equivalent: the digitization process led to a disconnection, due to the resolution of the discrete grid, not fine enough for catching the shape of X.

Gauss digitization [6], which is the intersection of a connected and bounded set X with $\mathbb{Z}^2$

$$X = X \cap \mathbb{Z}^2. \tag{1}$$

The digital object X is a finite subset of $\mathbb{Z}^2$; from an imaging point of view, it can be seen as a subset of pixels, *i.e.* unit squares defined as the Voronoi cells of the points of X within $\mathbb{R}^2$. The structure of X can be defined in various topological frameworks which are mainly equivalent [11] to that of digital topology [7]. However, digital topology of X is often non-coherent with continuous topology of X. This fact is illustrated in Fig. 2, where a connected continuous object X leads, after the Gauss digitization, to a disconnected digital object X. In the literature, various studies proposed conditions for guaranteeing the preservation of topology of digitized objects [9,20,21]. In particular, Pavlidis and Serra introduced the notion of *r-regularity*.

Definition 1 (*r*-regularity [17]). *An object* $X \subset \mathbb{R}^2$ *is r-regular if for each boundary point of* X, *there exist two open disks of radius* $r > 0$ *being tangent to the point, and lying entirely in* X *and its complement* $\overline{X}$, *respectively.*

Remark 1. The notion of *r*-regularity can be rewritten with morphological operators as follows: $X \subset \mathbb{R}^2$ is *r*-regular if

- $X \ominus B_r$ is non-empty and connected;
- $\overline{X} \ominus B_r$ is connected;
- $X = (X \ominus B_r) \oplus B_r$; and
- $\overline{X} = (\overline{X} \ominus B_r) \oplus B_r$,

where B_r denotes a closed disk of $\mathbb{R}^2$ of radius $r > 0$ and centered at $(0,0) \in \mathbb{R}^2$, $\oplus$ and $\ominus$ denote the classical operators of dilation and erosion, corresponding to the Minkowski addition and its associated subtraction:

$$X \oplus Y = \bigcup_{y \in Y} X_y = \bigcup_{x \in X} Y_x$$

$$X \ominus Y = \bigcap_{y \in Y} X_{-y}$$

with $X_y = \{x + y \mid x \in X\}$ and, in our case, $X, Y \subset \mathbb{R}^2$ [5,18,20].

It should be mentioned that this definition of r-regularity requires the boundary of X to be differentiable. More specifically, X must have a smooth contour with curvature at every point on the boundary is greater or equal to $\frac{1}{r}$. In addition, Pavlidis proved the topological equivalence of an r-regular object X and its digital counterpart X, for a dense sampling.

Proposition 1 ([17]). *An r-regular object* $X \subset \mathbb{R}^2$ *has the same topology as its digitized version* $X = X \cap \mathbb{Z}^2$ *if* $r \geq \frac{\sqrt{2}}{2}$.

To deal with non-regular objects, a notion called r-*halfregularity* has been proposed in [22]. More precisely, r-halfregular objects are defined as objects X having for each boundary point of X an open disk of radius $r > 0$ being tangent to the point, and lying entirely in either X or its complement $\overline{X}$. By definition, r-halfregular shapes are more general than r-regular ones since they include objects with non-differentiable boundary. Furthermore, it is shown that the r-halfregularity allows a topologically correct digitization of such an object using an additional repairing step. See [22] for more details.

2.2   Well-Composed Sets

To deal with topological paradoxes related to the discrete version of the Jordan theorem, a couple of dual adjacencies [19] are defined from the L^1 and L^∞ norms, leading to the well-known 4- and 8-adjacencies in $\mathbb{Z}^2$ [7]. More precisely, two distinct points $p, q \in \mathbb{Z}^2$, are k-adjacent if

$$\|p - q\|_\ell \leq 1 \tag{2}$$

with $k = 4$ (resp. 8) when $\ell = 1$ (resp. ∞). From the reflexive–transitive closure of the k-adjacency relation on a finite subset $X \subset \mathbb{Z}^2$, we derive the k-connectivity relation on X. It is an equivalence relation, whose equivalence classes are called the k-connected components of X. In order to avoid the topological issues of the Jordan theorem, dual adjacencies are used for X and its complement $\overline{X}$, namely $(4,8)$- or $(8,4)$-adjacencies [19]. Based on the digital topology framework, well-composedness has been introduced.

Definition 2 (Well-composed sets [8]). *We say that* X *is weakly well-composed if any 8-connected component of* X *is also a 4-connected component. We say that* X *is well-composed if both* X *and* $\overline{X}$ *are weakly well-composed.*

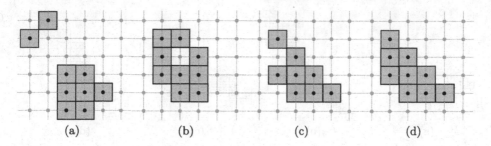

Fig. 3. (a) $X \subseteq \mathbb{Z}^2$ is neither connected nor well-composed. (b) X is weakly well-composed and $\overline{X}$ is 8-connected but not 4-connected. (c) $\overline{X}$ is weakly well-composed and X is 8-connected but not 4-connected. (d) X is 4-connected and well-composed.

This definition implies that the boundary[1] of X is a set of 1-manifolds whenever X is well-composed (see Fig. 3). In particular, there exists a strong link between r-regularity of $X \subset \mathbb{R}^2$ and well-composedness of $\mathsf{X} = X \cap \mathbb{Z}^2$.

Proposition 2 ([9]). *If $X \subset \mathbb{R}^2$ is r-regular, with $r \geq \frac{\sqrt{2}}{2}$, then $\mathsf{X} = X \cap \mathbb{Z}^2$ is well-composed.*

Well-composed sets present nice topological properties. However, they may be altered by rigid motions defined on $\mathbb{Z}^2$, as we will observe in the next section.

2.3   Digitized Rigid Motion and Topology Preservation

A rigid motion $\mathfrak{T}$ in $\mathbb{R}^2$ is defined for any point $\boldsymbol{x} = (x_1, x_2)^T$ as

$$\mathfrak{T}(\boldsymbol{x}) = \begin{pmatrix} \cos\theta & -\sin\theta \\ \sin\theta & \cos\theta \end{pmatrix} \begin{pmatrix} x_1 \\ x_2 \end{pmatrix} + \begin{pmatrix} t_1 \\ t_2 \end{pmatrix} \tag{3}$$

where $\theta \in [0, 2\pi)$ is a rotation angle, and $(t_1, t_2)^T \in \mathbb{R}^2$ is a translation vector.

The transformation $\mathfrak{T}$ is bijective, isometric and orientation-preserving. In other words, the transformation $\mathfrak{T}$ of a continuous object X in the Euclidean space $\mathbb{R}^2$, denoted by $\mathfrak{T}(X)$, has the same shape, *i.e.* the same geometry and topology, as X.

We cannot straightforwardly apply a rigid motion $\mathfrak{T}$, defined in Eq. (3), to a digital object $\mathsf{X} \subset \mathbb{Z}^2$, since we generally obtain a transformed object $\mathfrak{T}(\mathsf{X}) \not\subset \mathbb{Z}^2$. In order to obtain a result in $\mathbb{Z}^2$, we further need a digitization operator

$$\mathfrak{D} : \mathbb{R}^2 \to \mathbb{Z}^2 \tag{4}$$

which can be, for instance, the standard rounding function. Then, a digital analogue of $\mathfrak{T}$ can be defined as the composition of $\mathfrak{T}$, (restricted to $\mathbb{Z}^2$) with such digitization operator, as

$$\mathcal{T}_{point} = \mathfrak{D} \circ \mathfrak{T}_{|\mathbb{Z}^2}. \tag{5}$$

---

[1] The boundary of X is defined here as the boundary of the continuous object obtained as the union of the closed Voronoi cells associated to the points of X, in $\mathbb{R}^2$.

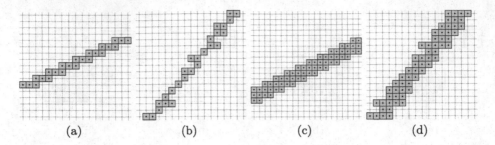

Fig. 4. Well-composed digital lines (a, c) with different thicknesses, which remain well-composed (d) or not (b) after a point-by-point digitized rigid motion $\mathcal{T}_{point}$. In both cases, the convexity of the digital lines is lost by $\mathcal{T}_{point}$ for the rotation angle of $\frac{\pi}{7}$ and the translation of $(\frac{1}{2}, \frac{1}{2})$.

Contrary to $\mathcal{T}$, $\mathcal{T}_{point}$ is, in general, neither injective nor surjective. In particular, the digitization $\mathfrak{D}$ may lead to unwanted results such as the topological and geometric properties of digital objects are changed by $\mathcal{T}_{point}$.

In this context, the issue of topological preservation of digital objects by $\mathcal{T}_{point}$ was investigated in [15]. A sufficient condition, namely *digital regularity*[2] was provided for guaranteeing that a well-composed digital object X will not be topologically modified by any arbitrary rigid motion $\mathcal{T}_{point}$.

However, this notion of digital regularity does not tackle the issue of geometry alteration. Indeed, the rigid motion model defined in Eq. (5) acts on the object in a point-wise way and does not preserve the shape of X. This is illustrated in Fig. 4 by digital lines with different thicknesses under $\mathcal{T}_{point}$. Though the initial shapes are very simple, the topology and geometry of digital objects are not always preserved.

3   Digital Shape Rigid Motions via Polygonization

3.1   Quasi-r-Regularity and Discrete Regularity

We now recall the notion of *quasi-r-regularity* for objects of $\mathbb{R}^2$ whose boundaries are not necessarily differentiable [14]. This notion provides sufficient conditions for preserving the connectivity by the Gaussian digitization.

Definition 3 (Quasi-r-regularity [14]). *Let* $X \subset \mathbb{R}^2$ *be a bounded and simply connected (i.e. connected with no hole) object. Let* $B_r \subset \mathbb{R}^2$ *be a closed disk of radius* $r > 0$. X *is said to be* quasi-r-regular, *if it satisfies*

(i) $X \ominus B_r$ *is non-empty and connected,*
(ii) $\overline{X} \ominus B_r$ *is connected,*
(iii) $X \subseteq (X \ominus B_r) \oplus B_{r\sqrt{2}}$, *and*
(iv) $\overline{X} \subseteq (\overline{X} \ominus B_r) \oplus B_{r\sqrt{2}}$.

---

[2] In [15] this notion was simply called *regularity*. We rename it as "digital regularity" to avoid the confusion with the continuous regularity, *i.e.* r-regularity, in Definition 1.

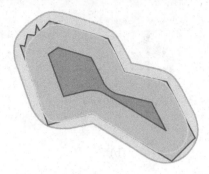

Fig. 5. A quasi-r-regular object X has its border included between $(X \ominus B_r) \oplus B_r$ and $(X \ominus B_r) \oplus B_{r\sqrt{2}}$. This is a counterexample of $P \subset \mathbb{R}^2$ (in blue) which is quasi-r-regular but does not satisfy the condition of Definition 4; both conditions of distance and angle at vertices are violated. $P \ominus B_r$ is in red, $(P \ominus B_r) \oplus B_r$ is bounded by the yellow curve and $(P \ominus B_r) \oplus B_{r\sqrt{2}}$ is in green. (Color figure online)

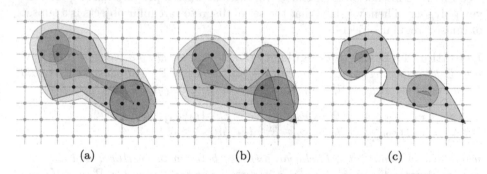

(a)   (b)   (c)

Fig. 6. Examples of quasi-1-regular (a) and non-quasi-1-regular (b,c) objects X: (b) $X \not\subseteq (X \ominus B_1) \oplus B_{\sqrt{2}}$; (c) $X \ominus B_1$ is not connected. The objects $X \subset \mathbb{R}^2$ are in blue, the disks B_1 are in red and the disks $B_{\sqrt{2}}$ are in black, the erosions $X \ominus B_1$ are in red and the openings $(X \ominus B_1) \oplus B_{\sqrt{2}}$ are in green. (Color figure online)

Roughly speaking, thanks to (*iii*), the border of X is included between $(X \ominus B_r) \oplus B_r$ and $(X \ominus B_r) \oplus B_{r\sqrt{2}}$. In other words, a *margin* of $(\sqrt{2}-1)r$ is authorized for the border of X (see Fig. 5). Examples of quasi-r-regular and non-quasi-r-regular objects are given in Fig. 6.

This notion of quasi-r-regularity provides sufficient conditions for guaranteeing that the connectedness of X will not be affected by the Gauss digitization process, as proven in [14].

Proposition 3 ([14]). *Let* $X \subset \mathbb{R}^2$ *be bounded and simply connected. If* X *is quasi-1-regular, then* $\mathsf{X} = X \cap \mathbb{Z}^2$ *is well-composed.*

In this article, we are interested in polygonal objects generated from the boundaries of digital objects of $\mathbb{Z}^2$. In the following, we introduce the notion of quasi-r-regularity restricted to polygons, namely *discrete-r-regularity*

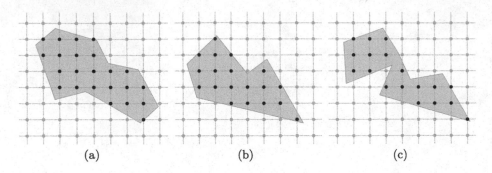

Fig. 7. Examples of discrete-1-regular (a) and non discrete-1-regular (b,c) polygons: (b) the condition of angle is violated and (c) both conditions of angle and distance are violated.

(see Fig. 7). This notion is extended from the definition proposed in [13] for convex polygons. Then, we show that the set of discrete-r-regular objects is a subset of quasi-r-regular objects.

Definition 4 (Discrete-r-regularity). *Let* P *be a simple polygon in* $\mathbb{R}^2$, *V and E be respectively the set of vertices and edges of* P. *The polygon* P *is said to be discrete-r-regular, if it satisfies the following two properties:*

(i) $\forall v = e_1 \cap e_2 \in V$ *with* $e_1, e_2 \in E$, $\forall e \in E \setminus \{e_1, e_2\}$, $d(v, e) \geq 2r$,
(ii) $\forall v = e_1 \cap e_2 \in V$ *with* $e_1, e_2 \in E$, $n(e_1).n(e_2) \geq 0$,

where $d(v, e)$ *denotes the Euclidean distance between the vertex* v *and the edge* e, $n(e)$ *denotes the normal vector of* e *directed to the exterior of* P, *and the dot "." designates the scalar product between two vectors.*

Roughly speaking, the polygon P is *discrete-r-regular* if, for any vertex $v \in V$, (*i*) v has a distance at least $2r$ to any edge that does not contain v, and (*ii*) the vertex angle at v is between $\frac{\pi}{2}$ and $\frac{3\pi}{2}$ (see Fig. 7).

Proposition 4. *Let* P $\subset \mathbb{R}^2$ *be a simple polygon. If* P *is discrete-r-regular, then* P *is quasi-r-regular.*

Proof. Assuming that P is discrete-r-regular, *i.e.* it satisfies the two conditions of Definition 4. We now prove that P is quasi-r-regular, *i.e.* it satisfies the four conditions of Definition 3. We only prove the conditions for P as the same reasoning holds for $\overline{P}$.

Consider the r-offset polygon of P, namely P $\ominus B_r$, which is defined by all interior points of P having a distance at least r from the boundary of P (see Fig. 8(a)). From (*i*) of Definition 4, any vertex v of P has its distance to any edge not containing v greater or equal to $2r$. Thus, P $\ominus B_r$ is non-empty and connected.

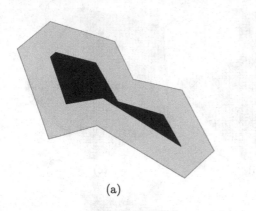

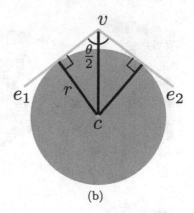

(a)   (b)

Fig. 8. (a) The r-offset polygon $P \ominus B_r$ (in black) of P (in blue). (b) Illustration for the proof of Proposition 4; $r \leq d(c, v) \leq r\sqrt{2}$ as $d(c, v) = \frac{r}{\sin(\frac{\theta}{2})}$ and $\frac{\pi}{2} \leq \theta \leq \frac{3\pi}{2}$. (Color figure online)

We now prove (iii) of Definition 3 by showing that $\forall v \in V$, the distance of v to $P \ominus B_r$ is between r and $r\sqrt{2}$. Let us consider a vertex $v = e_1 \cap e_2 \in V$ for $e_1, e_2 \in E$. Let $B_r(c)$ be the closed disk of radius r centered at c which is tangent to both e_1 and e_2 (see Fig. 8(b)). From the definition of erosion, c belongs to $P \ominus B_r$. We have $\sin \frac{\theta}{2} = \frac{r}{d(c,v)}$ where $d(c, v)$ is the Euclidean distance between c and v and θ is the angle at the vertex v, and thus $d(c, v) = \frac{r}{\sin \frac{\theta}{2}}$. Since $n(e_1).n(e_2) \geq 0$, $\frac{\pi}{2} \leq \theta \leq \frac{3\pi}{2}$, $\frac{\sqrt{2}}{2} \leq \sin \frac{\theta}{2} \leq 1$. This leads to $r \leq d(c, v) \leq r\sqrt{2}$.□

Note that the converse may not be true; a counterexample is given in Fig. 5. As exemplified in Figs. 6 and 7 as well, quasi-r-regular objects can have non-smooth boundaries (*i.e.* they can be non-differentiable), while discret-r-regular objects are restricted only to polygons.

The following corollary is a straightforward result of Proposition 4.

Corollary 1. *Let P be a simple polygon in $\mathbb{R}^2$ and E be the set of all edges of P. If P is discrete-r-regular, then $\forall e \in E$, $l(e) \geq 2r$ where $l(e)$ denotes the length of the edge e.*

Proposition 4 and Corollary 1 provide a sufficient condition of discrete-r-regular objects and allow for a geometric verification of such objects using the simple measures of angles and lengths of the considered polygons.

Remark 2. Previously, another discrete regularity defined specially for convex polygons was presented in [13]. The notion is based on the property on vertex angle, which is the same as (ii) in Definition 4, and on the existence of a ball of radius r tangent at each edge, which is contained in the polygon. Indeed, this last property is not as strong as (i) in Definition 4, so that it does not lead to the edge length property, as given in Corollary 1. Besides, the new notion given in Definition 4 is not restricted to convex polygons, and thus more general.

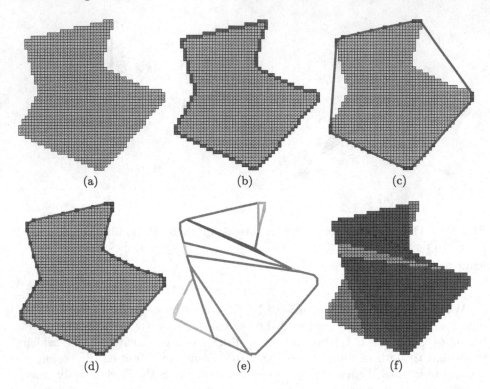

Fig. 9. (a) A digital shape X. (b) 8-connected contour $C(\mathsf{X})$ (in red) extracted from
(a). (c) Boundary of the convex hull (in blue) computed from $C(\mathsf{X})$. (d) Boundary of
the polygon $\mathsf{P}(\mathsf{X})$ (in green) of (a) based on the convex hull and $C(\mathsf{X})$ of X such that
$\mathsf{X} = \mathsf{P}(\mathsf{X}) \cap \mathbb{Z}^2$. (e) Decomposition into convex parts P_i of $\mathsf{P}(\mathsf{X})$ such that $\mathsf{P}(\mathsf{X}) =
\bigcup_{i=1..m} \mathsf{P}_i$. (f) Digital decomposition such that $\mathsf{X} = \mathsf{P}(\mathsf{X}) \cap \mathbb{Z}^2 = \bigcup_{i=1..m} \left(\mathsf{P}_i \cap \mathbb{Z}^2 \right)$.
(Color figure online)

3.2   Polygonization of a Digital Object and Convex Decomposition

We focus on a polygonal representation $\mathsf{P}(\mathsf{X})$ of a digital object X that satisfies
the following properties:

(i) Digitization reversibility: $\mathsf{P}(\mathsf{X}) \cap \mathbb{Z}^2 = \mathsf{X}$, and
(ii) Rationality: the vertices of $\mathsf{P}(\mathsf{X})$ have rational coordinates.

It should be mentioned that the second property is related to our framework
of digital geometry and exact computation. Indeed, we require the vertices of
$\mathsf{P}(\mathsf{X})$ to be rational points, and restrict the rigid motion $\mathfrak{T}$ to be rational, namely
rational rotations and rational translations. Thanks to this rational setting, the
vertices of $\mathfrak{T}(\mathsf{P}(\mathsf{X}))$ are also rational points. As a consequence, only exact computations with integers are involved. These assumptions do not cause applicative
restriction due to the finiteness of input set and the density of rational values
within the rotation and translation parameter space.

In order to compute the polygonal representation $P(X)$ which satisfies the above properties, we use the border points of X together with its convex hull. For an efficient computation of $P(X)$, we use the border tracing algorithm proposed in [4] and apply the discrete version of the Melkman algorithm [12] to compute the convex hull of the border points. Both methods have a linear time complexity w.r.t the number of border points.

The method of polygonal computation consists of first extracting the 8-connected contour points $C(X)$ of X, and then computing the convex hull of $C(X)$; see Fig. 9(b, c). We initialize the ordered vertex set V of the polygon P as the sequence of convex hull vertices. For any two consecutive vertices p_1 and p_2 of V, let us consider the set $C'(p_1, p_2) \subset C(X)$ of the contour points of X between p_1 and p_2. We select $p_3 \in C'(p_1, p_2) \setminus V$ such that

$$p_3 = \underset{q \in C'(p_1, p_2) \setminus V}{\arg\max} \left\{ d(p_1, q) \mid (\Delta p_1 q r \cap \mathbb{Z}^2) \cap \overline{X} = \emptyset \text{ for } r \in C'(p_1, q) \right\}$$

where $d(p_1, q)$ denotes the Euclidean distance between p_1 and q, and $\Delta p_1 q r$ is the triangle whose vertices are p_1, q and r. If such p_3 exists, we add it to V between p_1 and p_2. We repeat this process with V until no point is added, see Fig. 9(d). Note that convex hull vertices are also vertices of $P(X)$. We recall that one can use any other methods of polygonization to obtain $P(X)$ as far as the method is reversible and the vertices of the polygon have rational coordinates; for instance the approach based on digital straight segments proposed in [3] can be considered.

To perform a geometry-preserving rigid motion, we apply a convex decomposition to subdivide $P(X)$ into convex parts P_i, $i = 1..m$, (see Fig. 9) such that

$$P = \bigcup_{i=1..m} P_i. \tag{6}$$

Thus,

$$X = P(X) \cap \mathbb{Z}^2 = \left(\bigcup_{i=1..m} P_i \right) \cap \mathbb{Z}^2 = \bigcup_{i=1..m} (P_i \cap \mathbb{Z}^2). \tag{7}$$

In this work, we use the ACD (Approximate Convex Decomposition) algorithm proposed in [10]. The ACD method is based on a hierarchical strategy to perform the decomposition and has a $O(nr)$ complexity where n and r are the numbers of vertices and non-convex features of the polygon, respectively. We set the parameters of the ACD method to avoid any approximation of the convex decomposition. It should be mentioned that this step can be performed using the rational vertices of P. However, we use the convex decomposition since the digitization is simpler using the half-plane representation of each convex part than the direct digitization of a polygon.

3.3   Rigid Motion of Discrete-r-Regular Polygons

Before describing the rigid motion model that relies on a discrete-r-regular polygon P of $\mathbb{R}^2$ followed by a digitization process, we first explain the model for convex polygons proposed in [13] and then adapt it for non-convex ones using the convex decomposition (see Sect. 3.2).

A convex polygon $P \subset \mathbb{R}^2$ can be defined as the intersection of closed half-planes H as

$$P = \bigcap_{H \in \mathcal{R}(P)} H \tag{8}$$

where $\mathcal{R}(P)$ is the smallest set of closed half-planes that defines P. Each closed half-plane H of this subset is defined as

$$H = \{(x,y) \in \mathbb{R}^2 \mid ax + by + c \leq 0\}. \tag{9}$$

If P has rational vertices, then $a, b, c \in \mathbb{Q}$. These rational coefficients of H are obtained by a pair of consecutive vertices of P, denoted by $\mathsf{u}, \mathsf{v} \in \mathbb{Q}^2$, which are in the clockwise order, such that

$$(a, b) = (-w_y, w_x) \tag{10}$$
$$c = (a, b) \cdot \mathsf{u} \tag{11}$$

where $(w_x, w_y) = \mathsf{v} - \mathsf{u} \in \mathbb{Q}^2$. Then, a half-plane H, as defined in Eq. (9), is transformed by a rational rigid motion $\mathfrak{T}$ as

$$\mathfrak{T}(H) = \{(x,y) \in \mathbb{R}^2 \mid \alpha x + \beta y + \gamma \leq 0\} \tag{12}$$

where $\alpha, \beta, \gamma \in \mathbb{Q}$ are given by $(\alpha\ \beta)^T = R(a\ b)^T$ and $\gamma = c + \alpha t_1 + \beta t_2$. This leads to a rational half-plane. From Eqs. (9) and (12), we write the rigid motion $\mathfrak{T}$ of the convex polygon P as

$$\mathfrak{T}(P) = \mathfrak{T}\left(\bigcap_{H \in \mathcal{R}(P)} H\right) = \bigcap_{H \in \mathcal{R}(P)} \mathfrak{T}(H) \tag{13}$$

This rigid motion scheme can be extended to non-convex polygons via their convex decomposition. From Eqs. (7) and (13) we have

$$\mathfrak{T}(P) = \bigcup_{i=1..m} \mathfrak{T}(P_i) = \bigcup_{i=1..m} \left(\bigcap_{H \in \mathcal{R}(P_i)} \mathfrak{T}(H)\right) \tag{14}$$

If $P(X)$ is the polygon of a digital object X, $i.e.$ $X = P(X) \cap \mathbb{Z}^2$, then we define

$$\mathcal{T}_{Poly}(X) = \mathfrak{T}(P(X)) \bigcap \mathbb{Z}^2 = \bigcup_{i=1..m} \left(\mathfrak{T}(P_i) \bigcap \mathbb{Z}^2\right). \tag{15}$$

It has been proved in [14] that rigid motion via polygonal model allows us to preserve the 4-connectivity of the transformed object under the condition of quasi-1-regularity.

Proposition 5 ([14]). *If the polygon* P(X) *of a bounded and connected digital object* X *is quasi-1-regular, then* $\mathcal{T}_{\mathcal{P}oly}(X)$ *is 4-connected and well-composed.*

From Propositions 4 and 5, we have the corollary.

Corollary 2. *If the polygon* P(X) *of a bounded and connected digital object* X *is discrete-1-regular, then* $\mathcal{T}_{\mathcal{P}oly}(X)$ *is 4-connected and well-composed.*

In other words, if P(X) is discrete-1-regular, then $\mathcal{T}_{\mathcal{P}oly}(X)$, as defined in Eq. (15), preserves the topological property of the original object X. Furthermore, P(X) is a piecewise affine object of $\mathbb{R}^2$; thus it allows to approximate well the shape under the rigid motion. As a consequence, P(X) is processed in a topology- and geometry-preserving way by $\mathcal{T}_{\mathcal{P}oly}(X)$ for any $\mathcal{T}$ if P(X) satisfies the conditions in Definition 4.

4 Source Codes and Results

4.1 Download and Installation

The proposed method is implemented in C++ using the DGtal[3] open source library (Digital Geometry Tools and Algorithms). It is available at the github repository: https://github.com/ngophuc/RigidTransformAcd2D. The installation is done through classical cmake procedure[4] (see *INSTALLATION.txt* file).

4.2 Description and Usage

In the source codes, there are three packages:

- **polygonization** computes the polygon from a digital image (see Sect. 3.2), and the discrete-r-regularity is verified in this step for the computed polygon as well.
- **decomposeShapeAcd2d** decomposes a polygon into the convex parts using the ACD method[5] [10].
- **transformAConvexShape** implements the proposed rigid motion method (see Sect. 3.3).

The executable file is generated in the **build** directory and named **transformDecomShape2d**.

- **Input:** a binary image in pgm format contains a well-composed set.
- **Command line:** the execution is in the CODESOURCES/build. For example, to run the program on **image.pgm** with the name of the output file is **image_out.pgm**, the rigid motion with the parameter setting $t_x = 0.5$, $t_y = 0.3$, and $\theta = 0.78$ and the option **-r** to verify the discrete-1-regularity of the computed polygon, we use

---

[3] http://dgtal.org.
[4] http://www.cmake.org.
[5] The code sources are available at https://github.com/jmlien/acd2d.

```
./transformDecomShape2d -i image.pgm -o image_out.pgm -r
-a 0.5 -b 0.3 -t 0.78
```

More details about the options of the program can be found by the command line helper: `./transformDecomShape2d -h`

- **Output:** several files are generated as output (in pgm and svg format):

`image_out.pgm`	Output transformed image
`image_poly.svg`	Result of polygonization
`image_decomp.svg`	Result of convex decompostion
`image_shape.svg`	Result of digitized convex decomposition

It should be mentioned that the proposed method is supposed to perform with an exact computation with rational rigid motions. However, to simplify the model for the users, the code uses float numbers instead of rational numbers for approximating the rigid motions; in particular, the rotation angle parameter is given in radians.

Fig. 10. Left: input image, middle left: generated polygon with the convex decomposition from contour points, middle right: digitization via the convex decomposition, right: transformed results. For more details about rigid motion parameters of these experiments, see https://github.com/ngophuc/RigidTransformAcd2D.

4.3   Experimental Results

We now present some experiments on the convex decomposition for geometry-preserving rigid motions. It should be mentioned that the polygons generated from given digital sets are verified to be discrete-1-regular by the conditions in Definition 4. The results are shown in Fig. 10 with the center of rotations being the centroid of each set. Details of different parameters of rigid motions using for these experiments are found at the github repository: https://github.com/ngophuc/RigidTransformAcd2D.

5   Conclusion

This article presents a method for rigid motions of digital objects defined of $\mathbb{Z}^2$. More precisely, the method uses an intermediate model of a digital object, which is a polygon representing the digital object. Such polygon is continuous and processed by standard continuous transformations followed by a digitization to obtain a result in $\mathbb{Z}^2$. In particular, we proposed a notion of *discrete-r-regularity* for polygonal objects, and also showed that these objects are in a subset of *quasi-r-regular* objects [14]. It provides a sufficient condition for guaranteeing topological preservation when digitizing a polygonal object.

An online demonstration is available at http://ipol-geometry.loria.fr/~phuc/ipol_demo/DecompConvexRigidMotion, and the implementation of the method can be found at https://github.com/ngophuc/RigidTransformAcd2D.

References

1. Bazin, P.L., Pham, D.L.: Topology-preserving tissue classification of magnetic resonance brain images. IEEE Trans. Med. Imaging **26**, 487–496 (2007)
2. Bertrand, G., Everat, J.C., Couprie, M.: Image segmentation through operators based on topology. J. Electron. Imaging **6**, 395–405 (1997)
3. Dörksen-Reiter, H., Debled-Rennesson, I.: A linear algorithm for polygonal representations of digital sets. In: Reulke, R., Eckardt, U., Flach, B., Knauer, U., Polthier, K. (eds.) IWCIA 2006. LNCS, vol. 4040, pp. 307–319. Springer, Heidelberg (2006). https://doi.org/10.1007/11774938_24
4. Gonzalez, R.C., Woods, R.E.: Digital Image Processing, 3rd edn. Prentice-Hall Inc., Upper Saddle River (2006)
5. Heimans, H.J.A.M., Ronse, C.: The algebraic basis of mathematical morphology I. Dilations and erosions. Comput. Vis. Graph. Image Process. **50**(3), 245–295 (1990)
6. Klette, R., Rosenfeld, A.: Digital geometry: Geometric methods for digital picture analysis. Elsevier, Amsterdam (2004)
7. Kong, T.Y., Rosenfeld, A.: Digital topology: introduction and survey. Comput. Vis. Graph. Image Process. **48**(3), 357–393 (1989)
8. Latecki, L.J., Eckhardt, U., Rosenfeld, A.: Well-composed sets. Comput. Vis. Image Underst. **61**(1), 70–83 (1995)
9. Latecki, L.J., Conrad, C., Gross, A.: Preserving topology by a digitization process. J. Math. Imaging Vis. **8**(2), 131–159 (1998)

10. Lien, J.M., Amato, N.M.: Approximate convex decomposition of polygons. Comput. Geom. Theory Appl. **35**(1–2), 100–123 (2006)
11. Mazo, L., Passat, N., Couprie, M., Ronse, C.: Digital imaging: a unified topological framework. J. Math. Imaging Vis. **44**(1), 19–37 (2012)
12. Melkman, A.A.: On-line construction of the convex hull of a simple polyline. Inf. Process. Lett. **25**(1), 11–12 (1987)
13. Ngo, P., Kenmochi, Y., Debled-Rennesson, I., Passat, N.: Convexity-preserving rigid motions of 2D digital objects. In: Kropatsch, W.G., Artner, N.M., Janusch, I. (eds.) DGCI 2017. LNCS, vol. 10502, pp. 69–81. Springer, Cham (2017). https://doi.org/10.1007/978-3-319-66272-5_7
14. Ngo, P., Passat, N., Kenmochi, Y., Debled-Rennesson, I.: Geometric preservation of 2D digital objects under rigid motions. J. Math. Imaging Vis. **61**(2), 204–223 (2019)
15. Ngo, P., Passat, N., Kenmochi, Y., Talbot, H.: Topology-preserving rigid transformation of 2D digital images. IEEE Trans. Image Process. **23**(2), 885–897 (2014)
16. Ngo, P., Kenmochi, Y., Passat, N., Talbot, H.: Topology-preserving conditions for 2D digital images under rigid transformations. J. Math. Imaging Vis. **49**(2), 418–433 (2014)
17. Pavlidis, T.: Algorithms for Graphics and Image Processing. Springer, Berlin, Computer Science Press, Rockville (1982)
18. Ronse, C., Heimans, H.J.A.M.: The algebraic basis of mathematical morphology II. Dilations and erosions. Comput. Vis. Graph. Image Process. **54**(1), 74–97 (1990)
19. Rosenfeld, A.: Digital topology. Am. Math. Mon. **86**(8), 621–630 (1979)
20. Serra, J.: Image Analysis and Mathematical Morphology. Academic Press Inc., Orlando (1983)
21. Stelldinger, P., Köthe, U.: Towards a general sampling theory for shape preservation. Image Vis. Comput. **23**(2), 237–248 (2005)
22. Stelldinger, P., Terzic, K.: Digitization of non-regular shapes in arbitrary dimensions. Image Vis. Comput. **26**(10), 1338–1346 (2008). https://doi.org/10.1016/j.imavis.2007.07.013
23. Yilmaz, A., Javed, O., Shah, M.: Object tracking: a survey. ACM Comput. Surv. **38**(4), 1–45 (2006)
24. Zitová, B., Flusser, J.: Image registration methods: a survey. Image Vis. Comput. **21**(11), 977–1000 (2003)

Non-deterministic Behavior
of Ranking-Based Metrics When
Evaluating Embeddings

Anguelos Nicolaou[1,2(✉)], Sounak Dey[1], Vincent Christlein[2], Andreas Maier[2],
and Dimosthenis Karatzas[1]

[1] Computer Vision Center, Edificio O, Campus UAB, 08193 Bellaterra, Spain
{anguelos,sdey,dimos}@cvc.uab.cat
[2] Pattern Recognition Lab, Friedrich-Alexander-Universität Erlangen-Nürnberg,
Erlangen, Germany
{anguelos.nikolaou,vincent.christlein,andreas.maier}@fau.de

Abstract. Embedding data into vector spaces is a very popular strategy
of pattern recognition methods. When distances between embeddings
are quantized, performance metrics become ambiguous. In this paper,
we present an analysis of the ambiguity quantized distances introduce
and provide bounds on the effect. We demonstrate that it can have a
measurable effect in empirical data in state-of-the-art systems. We also
approach the phenomenon from a computer security perspective and
demonstrate how someone being evaluated by a third party can exploit
this ambiguity and greatly outperform a random predictor without even
access to the input data. We also suggest a simple solution making the
performance metrics, which rely on ranking, totally deterministic and
impervious to such exploits.

Keywords: Deterministic · mAP · Ranking ·
Performance evaluation · Word spotting · Precision · Recall ·
Adversarial

1 Introduction

1.1 Motivation

In typical pattern recognition works, researchers introduce algorithms and
demonstrate their performance using specific metrics.

The measure of difference between the obtained outputs and the given ideal
output (ground-truth) is the actual estimated performance. Although the exam-
ined systems can have some randomness, it is assumed they follow a statistical
distribution, whose mean can be estimated; it is generally also assumed that
measuring the difference from the ground-truth with metrics defined in the literature is purely deterministic. However, while experimenting with a typical
retrieval method, it occurred that a specific output from a system would yield

B. Kerautret et al. (Eds.): RRPR 2018, LNCS 11455, pp. 71–82, 2019.
https://doi.org/10.1007/978-3-030-23987-9_5

different measured performances when evaluated with data in a different order. After investigation, the problem was found to be a form of numerical instability, possibly attributed to the 32 bit limitation of modern GPU computing. The problem is quite general and affects performance evaluation metrics that require sorting distances matrices. In this paper, we (1) reproduce the incoherence in the recorded behavior of a real-world system, (2) we provide a data-driven analysis of the phenomenon, and (3) provide a simple fix that provably makes ranking-based metrics, such as mean average precision (mAP) [6], behave deterministically under these conditions.

1.2   Performance Evaluation and Competitions

Evaluation protocols are a sensitive matter. As there is no way to assess them objectively, their validity is mostly determined by consensus on how informative they are. In order to constrain experimental bias, the development of a system and evaluating a system is considered as two distinct acts and researchers always try to keep the two roles as distinct as possible. In the case of competitions, the two roles are strictly segregated between participants and organizers. For such reasons, competitions set the gold standard in performance evaluation and have gained popularity. As an indication of the rising popularity and importance of competitions, in the context of ICDAR in 2017, 25 different competitions were hosted by different groups while ten years earlier in 2007, there were only 3. Competitions establish a good practice in performance evaluation, which people then apply to measure their own methods' performance.

2   Rank Based Metrics

Most of the popular performance metrics associated with Information Retrieval (IR) are closely related among each other. In the most usual form, IR systems return data from a database sorted by relevance with respect to a query sample. Then, evaluation metrics are computed that assess the ranking.

Any classification problem can be considered a retrieval problem where all samples in the database having the same class as the query are the relevant documents. In this way, ranking metrics have become prevalent in evaluating classification tasks.

2.1   Metric Estimation

The first step in computing ranking metrics of an embedding is to compute the distance matrix $D \in \mathbb{R}^{Q \times K}$ between any query $x_q, q \in \{1, \ldots, Q\}$ and a database of size K for a specified distance metric, or equivalently a similarity matrix. The next step is to compute a relevance matrix $R \in \{0, 1\}^{Q \times K}$ with elements:

$$R_{q,k} = \begin{cases} 1 & \text{if } y(x_q) = y(x_d) \\ 0 & \text{if } y(x_q) \neq y(x_d) \end{cases}, \tag{1}$$

where $y(x)$ denotes the class of sample x.

The row-wise sorting of R by the values in D, results in the so called *correct matrix* $C \in \mathbb{R}^{Q \times K}$, containing elements that are 1 if the k-th closest sample of the database to the query q is relevant and 0 otherwise. The matrix C can be directly used to compute the precision and recall for any query x_q and rank k resulting in the matrix Pr and Rc, respectively with elements:

$$Pr_{q,k} = \frac{1}{k} \sum_{n=1}^{k} C_{q,n} \qquad Rc_{q,k} = \frac{\sum_{n=1}^{k} C_{q,n}}{\sum_{n=1}^{} C_{q,n}} . \qquad (2)$$

These two matrices can be used to produce all established metrics such as mean Average Precision (mAP), precision at rank 10, accuracy etc. In the remaining of this paper we focus on mAP as it is by far the most popular of these metrics but the observations and analysis can easily be extended to all such metrics.

2.2 Performance Evaluation of Embeddings

A deployable retrieval system can be defined as a system that ranks a database of samples with respect to a query sample. In most cases, retrieval systems consist of two steps: (1) mapping samples into a representation, i. e., typically a vector of fixed dimensionality and (2) returning the distance of the two representations. Embedding methods map any sample to a metric space $\mathbb{R}^n$ and usually used in combination with a metric distance, such as Euclidean distance, to form a retrieval system.

Performance evaluation protocols should be designed such any person acts either as a *creator* (of a method) or an *evaluator* (of the method) at any given time. It follows that the test-set should not be accessible to the creator, Ideally, the only thing the creator should pass to the evaluator is an opaque system (black-box) that produces outputs for given inputs and the evaluator should run this system on sequestered data and return a performance score. The aforementioned is the higher standard for performance evaluation. Yet, quite often, the creator receives the test samples and reports the outputs instead of providing his system as a black-box; yet any evaluation protocol should be designed so that it can accommodate the strict separation of creator and evaluator.

The question arises, where does the retrieval system end and where does the evaluation system begin? Under the assumption that the embedding method has a high cost, from an evaluators perspective, it is a lot faster to compute all the embeddings in the test-set only once, and then compute the distance matrix of them given a distance metric. The other alternative, ranking the database for every query sample independently, would cost a lot more and is practically intractable, because for each query, the embeddings for the database are recomputed.

In terms of complexity, assuming the number of queries and the size of the retrieval database to be of approximately the sane size m, the dimensionality of the embedding to be a constant and the cost of mapping a single sample as k, then the complexity of a performance evaluation for systems with ranked outputs can be given by:

$$\mathcal{O}(k \times m \times m) = \mathcal{O}(km^2) \tag{3}$$

On the other hand, under the assumption that the embedding dimensionality n is a constant, the complexity for evaluating a black-box producing embeddings is given by:

$$\mathcal{O}(k \times m + k \times m + m \times m) = \mathcal{O}(max(m^2, km)) \tag{4}$$

The aforementioned computability issue is not only theoretical, it is also well exemplified in the evolution the writer identification competition from ICHFR 2012 [8] to ICDAR 2013 [7] where the increase of the test set made the transition inevitable The above problem is not just about evaluating, retrieval methods, such as word-spotting with dynamic time-warping [10], are not tractable for large-scale retrieval systems due to their computational complexity. Embedding methods ensure a tractable computational complexity for retrieval system and thus, they are so important.

2.3 Equidistant Samples

When sorting is part of the evaluation protocol, each sorting of the database that affects the ranking of relevant samples must be deterministic and unambiguous. If rows in the distance matrix contain duplicate distances, then ranking becomes undefined. Important to note is that an undefined algorithmic behavior in the context of sorting, is not the same as a random one. As opposed to random behavior, we cannot obtain an estimate of the expectation by repeatedly running the algorithm. Worse than that, undefined behavior might behave deterministically with respect to unknown and theoretically irrelevant factors, such as the order of the queries or even memory availability. This allows for bugs that are hard to detect and hard to be reproduced.

In Fig. 1 the problem and the effect equidistant samples in the database have on the resulting mAP is demonstrated. Line (a) is an indicative retrieval given a query where the relevant data appears in the first and sixth position. Line (b) represents a perfect retrieval case, which obtains an AP of 100%. Lines (c) to (f) represent alternative sorting of the same embeddings where the first two samples and the fifth to seventh samples are equidistant from the query. As can be seen, ambiguity only occurs when consecutive equidistant samples are both relevant (green) and non relevant (non-green).

Other metrics depending on sorting are also affected to an equivalent degree, but we focus on mAP because it is the most popular metric.

3   Experimental Data Analysis

3.1   PHOCNET

Although this paper addresses the general case of vector embeddings, we show experimental validation using a specific retrieval task known as segmented

	Query	Alternative Retrievals ranked by distance	Average Precision
a)	0	1 2 3 4 5 6 7 8 9... 99 100	66.66 %
b)	0	1 2 3 4 5 6 7 8 9... 99 100	100 %
c)	0	1 1 3 4 5 5 5 8 9... 99 100	70 %
d)	0	1 1 3 4 5 5 5 8 9... 99 100	39.28 %
e)	0	1 1 3 4 5 5 5 8 9... 99 100	64.28 %
f)	0	1 1 3 4 5 5 5 8 9... 99 100	45 %

Fig. 1. mAP calculated for a query where there are 2 relevant samples out of 100 in the database. Green boxes are the relevant samples, non-green colored boxes are samples of other classes, while gray boxes signify irrelevant boxes whose class doesn't matter. Red borders denote clusters of samples that are equidistant from the query. (Color figure online)

word-spotting. Segmented word-spotting classifies a word-image into word classes, i.e., elements of a dictionary. Word-spotting is quite often modeled as a typical embedding system used in the context of information retrieval. Domain adaptation has been a popular strategy, allowing to learn embeddings which map both word-images and word-transcriptions into a common subspace, the Pyramid Histogram Of Characters (PHOC) [2].

The PHOCNET [12] is a deep CNN, which is trained with a regression loss to map word-image inputs to a PHOC space ($\mathbb{R}^{504}$). The PHOC space is a metric space under the cosine distance. For evaluation, we use the George Washington (GW) dataset [5]. Specifically, we evaluate the test-set in a leave-one-out-image out cross-evaluation, i.e., each sample of the test set is compared with the remainder of the test-set. The test-set is stemmed for short (3 characters or less), and numerals so that there are 1164 word images left belonging to 431 classes. Singleton samples, samples that occur only once and therefore can not be both a query and in the retrieval database, are removed from the query set, which is reduced to 899 samples, but are retained in retrieval database. In Fig. 2 the distribution of collisions under different distance metrics is shown.

A collision refers to two samples in the database having exactly the same distance. For visualization purposes, this was extended to all distances smaller than a threshold ϵ in Figs. 2 and 3. Note, for a better visualization, the first 650 samples are dropped from the test-set. When measuring the mAP of retrieval with GW, we observed values between 95.34% and 95.36% attributed to equidistant samples.

3.2   Random Embeddings

We perform an additional experiment to obtain further insights and contextualize the measurements on GW. We generated white noise embeddings of exactly the same cardinality as the PHOCNET embeddings uniformly sampled in the range [0, 1] having the same range as the PHOCNET embeddings. We also used

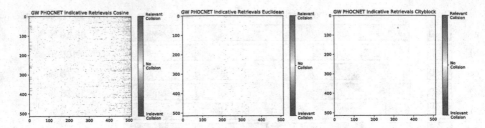

Fig. 2. PHOCNET embeddings for GW under various distances with $\epsilon = 10^{-10}$. Rows represent queries and columns represent samples sorted from left to right by similarity to each query.

the same labels as GW test-set to make sure that the labeling statistics are identical. In Fig. 3 we can see occurrence of collisions under different distance metrics. In order to visualize collisions, we considered any consecutive samples having a difference greater than ϵ as colliding. In the case of random embeddings, in order to produce enough collisions to have plots comparable to GW we had to increase ϵ to 10^{-6}.

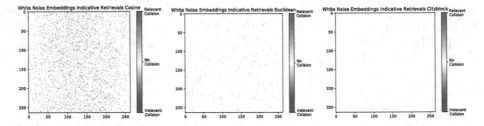

Fig. 3. Random embeddings with the same cardinalities and labels as GW. Rows represent queries and columns represent samples sorted from left to right by similarity to each query.

3.3   Analysis

These experiments[1] provide some insights into the described phenomena. What stands out is the effect the different distance functions have on the same vectors. Specifically it is worth observing that consistently across both GW and random embeddings, city-block distance produces a lot less collisions than Euclidean distance which in turn has approximately 20 times less collisions than cosine distance. Conversely, it is worth pointing out that only in the case of the trained embeddings and cosine distance almost all collisions happen in the right side of the spectrum, where samples that are the furthest apart from each query concentrate. Furthermore, PHOCNET in combination with cosine distance produces

---

[1] All experiments and plots presented in this paper are reproducible and available at https://github.com/anguelos/embedding_map.

many collisions among relevant samples. This demonstrates the extent to which PHOCNET manages to regress perfect PHOC representations. Another important observation is that in order to produce plots where collisions are visible when using random embeddings we had to increase the collision visibility criterion from 10^{-10} to 10^{-5}. The fact that a real-world method is 10000 times more prone to collisions than random data of the same cardinalities and distributions is a good indication that the probability of collision is practically unpredictable unless measured.

4   Proposed Solution

4.1   Determinism and Bounds

The principal problem arising from equidistant embeddings is the unpredictability of their sorting. The simplest remedy for this is to make the evaluation system consistently sort equidistant samples in the most favorable way possible. Therefore, we define a new matrix E, which holds a small constant ϵ for any non-relevant element:

$$E = (1 - R) * \epsilon , \tag{5}$$

where R is the relevance matrix R, cf. Sect. 2.1. Then, we can define two new similarity/distance matrices D^+ and D^- as:

$$D^+ = D + E \qquad D^- = D - E . \tag{6}$$

In this way, the relevant and irrelevant matches are separated from each other. Note, collisions within the individual groups have no influence on the performance evaluation.

In order to only affect equidistant samples, ϵ must be smaller than the smallest observed difference between any pair of distances in any query that is greater than zero.[2]

It follows that computing mAP from D^+ instead of D, provides an upper bound on all the plausible mAP estimates for given outputs of a system. Respectively, by computing mAP from D^-, we can get the lower bound among all plausible mAP estimates of the performance of a system. From here on we refer to the two bounds as mAP$^+$ and mAP$^-$. Figure 4 shows D and E computed on a part of the GW test-set. It should be pointed out that the modality used is self-classification, where queries and database are the same samples, and the nearest sample to each query is always omitted as the sample is always itself with a distance of 0. Given the small numerical effect equidistant samples have over the mAP in real world systems, providing the two bounds of mAP should be informative enough. It should be pointed out that both bounds are deterministic with respect to the embeddings and the data labels, and therefore also their mean. Nonetheless, the mean of the bounds is not directly related to the expected AP of a retrieval containing equidistant samples.

---

[2] This can for example be easily achieved by switching from float to double precision and choosing ϵ appropriately.

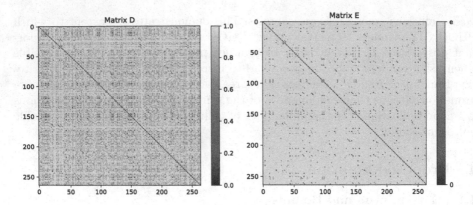

Fig. 4. Cosine distance matrix D for the GW test-set and the matrix E.

4.2   Expectation

While the bounds of all valid mAP are easy to compute, computing the expected mAP over all possible permutations of equidistant samples is not trivial.

As can be seen in Fig. 1 an ambiguous ranking contains one, or more sequences of equidistant samples that are both relevant and non-relevant.

By definition mAP only samples precision at the points where recall changes, thus equidistant sequences with only relevant or non-relevant sequences do not affect mAP and can be ignored. It can also be deduced that the effect each sequence of equidistant samples has over the total mAP expectation can be independently computed for every equidistant sequence.

Each equidistant sequence of length l containing m relevant samples, is preceded by a retrieval of n relevant samples from k retrieved samples. We then know that precision before the sequence is n/k and after it is $(n + m)/(k + l)$. The two fractions $(n+m)/(k+m)$ and $(n)/(k+l-m)$ are respectively the upper and lower bounds of all possible precision measurements occurring within the equidistant sequence. By definition of the mAP, we also know that each equidistant sequence will affect the overall mAP m times, thus m is in effect a coefficient of the sequence. Under the assumption of small equidistant sequences, the mean mAP for all possible permutations of equidistant samples could be computed but the brute force algorithm would be inefficient.

5   Exploitation of the Unpredictability

5.1   A Computer Security Approach

Although scientific work is predicated on the integrity of the scientists, it is important to keep in mind that there might be serious incentives for improving the perceived performance of a system. The disqualification [1] of Baidu from the ImageNet competition [11] demonstrates that even the leading scientific teams can show ambiguous ethics. More than that, the incident is an interesting example of how a participant to a competition can act in a manner that is ethically in a gray-zone rather than all-out cheating. Performance evaluation design in the context of public competitions should have a computer security aspect to it, the rules and protocols should be designed in a way that ethical gray-zones are minimized. People could always cheat or lie, but most people, will never cross that line.

5.2   All Zero Embedding Exploit

Even though the experiments presented in Sect. 3 demonstrate that the phenomenon of sorting ambiguity has a small effect under regular conditions, there are circumstances where it could be exploited and amplified the effect to an extreme level.

As a naive exploitation of the ambiguity we tried the following adversarial example. We hypothesized a system that always maps any input sample to a vector of $\mathbb{R}^{1000}$ with all zeros. When all embeddings have all zeros, then everything is equidistant. All performance estimates depend on how the sorting algorithm deals with equal values. We created labels for a thousand samples, 10 classes each having 100 samples. Afterwards, we employed standard self-classification where query and retrieval samples are the same, also known as leave-one-out cross-validation. By tweaking the order in which we evaluated the samples, which were identical, we managed to obtain different mAP measurements between 10.32% and 18.68%. In Fig. 5, the sample arrangements that produce the most and least favorable mAP estimates are visible. The exploit does not produce the full range of mAP^- to mAP^+, which lies in the range 5.18% to 100%. In order to produce such a variation, someone would probably need to alter the distance matrix D instead of the order of the queries. The exploit was not demonstrated on publicly deployed system but rather on a straight forward implementation of mAP as described in Sect. 2.1. The exploit is simpler to implement in leave-one-evaluation is also directly applicable to regular retrieval if the retrieval samples are sorted by class or if the third party being evaluated can infer how order of the samples relates to their classes.

It should be pointed out that over 30 repetitions of random embeddings instead of all zero produced an mAP mean of 10.4% with a standard deviation of 0.053%. The repercussions of this finding are quite significant as the adversarial all-zero system managed to outperform almost by two-fold the random system. There are many cases where systems are considered state-of-the-art while marginally surpassing the random predictor. For example, in gender identification from handwriting [4] the winner [9] demonstrated a performance of 62% while the random predictor produces 50%.

5.3   Protection from the Exploit

From the perspective of securing mAP against attacks exploiting equidistant samples, the simplest solution is to substitute mAP with mAP^-. Adopting

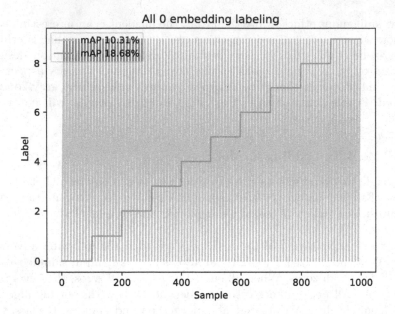

Fig. 5. Most favorable and least favorable orderings of the query samples.

mAP^- as the evaluation metric puts a penalty on equidistant samples without any foreseeable side-effect. If someone being evaluated wants to be protected from map^- having a penalty on him, he can easily avoid it by adding some noise on his outputs. Given that equidistant samples occur rarely in regular conditions, having them in such abundance so that they affect the evaluation metrics significantly, should probably be attributed to intent or poor system design. In either case this should not be rewarded. The last but most important reason for adopting mAP^- instead of mAP, is that no system that is agnostic to the inputs should ever out-perform a random predictor significantly.

6   Conclusion

6.1   Key Points

The key points and arguments of this paper can be summarized as follows:

- Randomness is allowed in evaluated systems but should not be accepted in evaluation metrics.
- Unpredictability of an algorithm should not be treated as randomness.
- Evaluation protocols should be treating systems as black boxes.
- Embedding methods scale well large datasets and are the most applicable pattern recognition retrieval techniques.
- Evaluation of embeddings requires sorting the distances from the query.
- Relevant and non-relevant samples that are equidistant from the query make the exact mAP measurement unpredictable.

- Although marginal, this phenomenon has been observed in real-world systems.
- The unpredictability can be easily addressed but estimating the "True" mAP is more complicated.
- The phenomenon can be used malevolently to demonstrate performance significantly better than the random predictor while totally independent from input data.
- In the context of competitions and other rigorous testing, mAP^- should be preferred over mAP as it penalizes the occurrence of ambiguities and motivates the method's creator to resolve them.

6.2   Discussion

The collision effect from equidistant samples in real scenarios is rather small, but it should be pointed out that detecting such phenomena in most circumstances is practically impossible. Therefore, we cannot really know how often they occur. The fact that GPUs, which are used in practically all modern pattern recognition methods, operate on 32 bit floating point, makes equidistant sample ambiguity more plausible. Moreover, embedding methods might produce near-discretized embeddings, such as the PHOC, or even discretized ones, such as POOF [3]. This makes the occurrence of such phenomena even more probable than one would expect. We believe that an evaluation metric should be robust against adversarial inputs and always provide meaningful results. We also believe that the standard of reproducibility, to which an evaluation metric is set, should be higher than any other component of the experimental evaluation. While one might argue that it is hard to prove the statistical significance of the analyzed phenomena, we believe that performance metrics should be held to the standard of algebra. It can be argued that statistics are not as informative when analyzing phenomena such as numerical instability. Numerical instability problems cannot be modeled as random variables because they are usually pseudo-deterministic; a system will usually be extremely consistent in producing the wrong number, thus repetition cannot provide an estimation on the distribution that the instability follows.

Computer and data science operates in a totally deterministic space where all randomness seizes at the point of digitization. When the behavior of systems modeled black-boxes is the subject of scientific analysis, then the actual evaluation metrics are the principal mean of observation, it is important to know and control the exact amount of error that these metrics have. Disparities on measurements of the same observation must be quantified, accounted for, and understood, as in many cases, one might be right to suspect they indicate a bug in his experimental pipeline.

By considering only statistically significant errors in the metrics as unacceptable, we let go of perfect reproducibility.

By providing an easily computable quantification of these effects, we remove this source of non-determinism from an otherwise purely deterministic experimental process.

Acknowledgments. This work has been partially supported by the European fund for regional development, grant-nr. 211 and the Spanish project TIN2017-89779-P. The contents of this publication are the sole responsibility of the authors.

References

1. Chinese search giant Baidu disqualified from AI test. British Broadcasting Corporation (BBC), June 2016. https://www.bbc.com/news/technology-33005728
2. Almazán, J., Gordo, A., Fornés, A., Valveny, E.: Word spotting and recognition with embedded attributes. IEEE Trans. Pattern Anal. Mach. Intell. **36**(12), 2552–2566 (2014)
3. Berg, T., Belhumeur, P.: POOF: part-based one-vs.-one features for fine-grained categorization, face verification, and attribute estimation. In: 2013 IEEE Conference on Computer Vision and Pattern Recognition, pp. 955–962 (2013)
4. Djeddi, C., Al-Maadeed, S., Gattal, A., Siddiqi, I., Souici-Meslati, L., El Abed, H.: ICDAR2015 competition on multi-script writer identification and gender classification using QUWI database. In: 2015 13th International Conference on Document Analysis and Recognition (ICDAR), pp. 1191–1195. IEEE (2015)
5. Fischer, A., Keller, A., Frinken, V., Bunke, H.: Lexicon-free handwritten word spotting using character HMMs. Pattern Recognit. Lett. **33**(7), 934–942 (2012)
6. Larson, R.R.: Introduction to information retrieval. J. Am. Soc. Inf. Sci. Technol. **61**(4), 852–853 (2010)
7. Louloudis, G., Gatos, B., Stamatopoulos, N., Papandreou, A.: ICDAR 2013 competition on writer identification. In: 2013 12th International Conference on Document Analysis and Recognition (ICDAR), pp. 1397–1401. IEEE (2013)
8. Louloudis, G., Gatos, B., Stamatopoulos, N.: ICFHR 2012 competition on writer identification challenge 1: Latin/Greek documents. In: 2012 International Conference on Frontiers in Handwriting Recognition (ICFHR), pp. 829–834. IEEE (2012)
9. Nicolaou, A., Bagdanov, A.D., Liwicki, M., Karatzas, D.: Sparse radial sampling LBP for writer identification. In: 2015 13th International Conference on Document Analysis and Recognition (ICDAR), pp. 716–720. IEEE (2015)
10. Rath, T.M., Manmatha, R.: Word image matching using dynamic time warping. In: 2003 IEEE Computer Society Conference on Computer Vision and Pattern Recognition, vol. 2, pp. 521–527. IEEE (2003)
11. Russakovsky, O., et al.: Imagenet large scale visual recognition challenge. Int. J. Comput. Vis. **115**(3), 211–252 (2015)
12. Sudholt, S., Fink, G.A.: PHOCNet: a deep convolutional neural network for word spotting in handwritten documents. In: 2016 15th International Conference on Frontiers in Handwriting Recognition (ICFHR), pp. 277–282. IEEE (2016)

RRPR Short Papers

CNN Implementation for Semantic Heads Segmentation Using Top-View Depth Data in Crowded Environment

Rocco Pietrini[✉], Daniele Liciotti, Marina Paolanti, Emanuele Frontoni, and Primo Zingaretti

Department of Information Engineering (DII), Universitá Politecnica delle Marche, Via Brecce Bianche, 12, 60131 Ancona, Italy
{r.pietrini,d.liciotti,m.paolanti}@pm.univpm.it,
{e.frontoni,p.zingaretti}@univpm.it

Abstract. The paper "Convolutional Networks for semantic Heads Segmentation using Top-View Depth Data in Crowded Environment" [1] introduces an approach to track and detect people in cases of heavy occlusions based on CNNs for semantic segmentation using top-view RGB-D visual data. The purpose is the design of a novel U-Net architecture, U-Net 3, that has been modified compared to the previous ones at the end of each layer. In order to evaluate this new architecture a comparison has been made with other networks in the literature used for semantic segmentation. The implementation is in Python code using Keras API with Tensorflow library. The input data consist of depth frames, from Asus Xtion Pro Live OpenNI recordings (.oni). The dataset used for training and testing of the networks has been manually labeled and it is freely available as well as the source code. The aforementioned networks have their stand-alone Python script implementation for training and testing. A Python script for the on-line prediction in OpenNI recordings (.oni) is also provided. Evaluation of the networks has been made with different metrics implementations (precision, recall, F1 Score, Sørensen-Dice coefficient), included in the networks scripts.

Keywords: CNN · People detection · Top-view

1 Introduction

The main novelty in this work is to take an existing convolutional neural network architecture initially born for medical image segmentation [2] and use it, after a proper training phase, for head detection in a top-view depth frame. In order to evaluate the new architecture on our application domain, that is people counting in heavy crowded environment, a new dataset has been built and freely published. After a first evaluation of the networks present in the literature we modified U-Net architecture to achieve better performances.

The paper is organized as follows: Sect. 2 introduces our approach consisting of a modified U-Net and gives details on the "TVHeadsDataset" [3]. Section 3 presents conclusions with future works.

© Springer Nature Switzerland AG 2019
B. Kerautret et al. (Eds.): RRPR 2018, LNCS 11455, pp. 85–88, 2019.
https://doi.org/10.1007/978-3-030-23987-9_6

2   Implementation

2.1   Dataset

The dataset consist of 1815 (320 × 240 pixels) 16-bit depth images, acquired in real scenarios. Binary masks indicating heads in the frame as ground truth are also provided. The labeling has been manually made by 6 human annotator with a majority policy. Additionally 8-bit images, obtained from the original one through conversion, have been used for comparing purpose, as they allow to enhance the overall contrast.

The first step is the image management, for this reason we created a script `data.py` in charge of pre-process each image with resizing, split the dataset in train and validation and store them in Numpy binary format for faster loading.

2.2   State of the Art

The first step was to implement different architectures taken from the literature. FractalNet [4], U-Net [2], U-Net2 [5], SegNet [6], ResNet [7] has been implemented. Source code is implemented through Keras 2 functional API, with a specific script for training and testing each network and also a script for on line prediction with U-Net 3. Sørensen-Dice coefficient has been selected as loss function minimizing the negative Dice loss, in a total of 200 epochs, with the Adam optimizer. In order to evaluate the networks each script contains implementations for the following metrics: Sørensen-Dice coefficient, accuracy, precision, recall, f1 score. In the original paper has been also calculated the Jaccard index from the Sørensen-Dice coefficient.

2.3   U-Net 3

The network architecture is depicted in Fig. 1, basically we started from U-Net classic architecture with the main idea to add a batch normalization after the first ReLU activation function and after each max-pooling and up-sampling functions.

The main contribution is contained in script `train_unet3_conv.py` that after loading the dataset using the aforementioned functions implement the network for training and testing. Final results are then stored in csv files for both 8 and 16 bit images.

2.4   On-Line Prediction

The dedicated script for the on-line prediction takes a OpenNI recording file (.oni) as argument and after loading the trained model predict on line the semantic segmentation frame by frame, saving the predicted binary images.

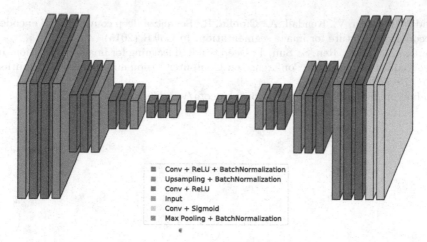

Conv + ReLU + BatchNormalization
Upsampling + BatchNormalization
Conv + ReLU
Input
Conv + Sigmoid
Max Pooling + BatchNormalization

Fig. 1. U-Net 3 architecture.

3 Conclusion

People counting from top view cameras allow to avoid problems like occlusion and can be reduced to head counting problem, with the obvious advantage that from an image point of view blobs (heads) unlikely will overlap or touch themselves, bringing high performances [8]. Semantic segmentation is the first step of every counting and tracking algorithm and our approach show great performance in terms of accuracy and speed for top-view depth images. In the later steps will be really trivial to implement a contour detection and tracking, since we already have a binary image, that can also be used as masks to retrieve the depth information. The aforementioned scripts allow to reproduce all the experiments in the original paper, in particular tables I and II [1] regarding Sørensen-Dice coefficient, while the relative Jaccard can be directly calculated from it.

References

1. Liciotti, D., Paolanti, M., Pietrini, R., Frontoni, E., Zingaretti, P.: Convolutional networks for semantic heads segmentation using top-view depth data in crowded environment. In: 2018 24th International Conference on Pattern Recognition (ICPR)
2. Ronneberger, O., Fischer, P., Brox, T.: U-net: convolutional networks for biomedical image segmentation. In arXiv preprint. arXiv:1505.04597 (2015)
3. Dataset. http://vrai.dii.univpm.it/tvheads-dataset
4. Larsson, G., Maire, M., Shakhnarovich, G.: Fractalnet: ultra-deep neural networks without residuals. In arXiv preprint. arXiv:1605.07648 (2016)
5. Ravishankar, H., Venkataramani, R., Thiruvenkadam, S., Sudhakar, P., Vaidya, V.: Learning and incorporating shape models for-semantic segmentation. In: Descoteaux, M., Maier-Hein, L., Franz, A., Jannin, P., Collins, D.L., Duchesne, S. (eds.) MICCAI 2017. LNCS, vol. 10433, pp. 203–211. Springer, Cham (2017). https://doi.org/10.1007/978-3-319-66182-7_24

6. Badrinarayanan, V., Kendall, A., Cipolla, R.: Segnet: a deep convolutional encoder-decoder architecture for image segmentation. In CoRR (2015)
7. He, K., Zhang, X., Ren, S., Sun, J.: Deep residual learning for image recognition. In: Proceedings of the IEEE Conference on Computer Vision and Pattern Recognition, pp. 770–778 (2016)
8. Online prediction. https://www.youtube.com/watch?v=MWjcW-3A5-I

Connected Components Labeling on DRAGs: Implementation and Reproducibility Notes

Federico Bolelli[✉], Michele Cancilla, Lorenzo Baraldi, and Costantino Grana

Dipartimento di Ingegneria "Enzo Ferrari", Università degli Studi di
Modena e Reggio Emilia, Via Vivarelli 10, 41125 Modena, MO, Italy
{federico.bolelli,michele.cancilla,lorenzo.baraldi,
costantino.grana}@unimore.it

Abstract. In this paper we describe the algorithmic implementation
details of "Connected Components Labeling on DRAGs" (Directed
Rooted Acyclic Graphs), studying the influence of parameters on the
results. Moreover, a detailed description of how to install, setup and use
YACCLAB (Yet Another Connected Components LAbeling Benchmark)
to test DRAG is provided.

1   Introduction

Connected Components Labeling (CCL) is one of the fundamental operations
in Computer Vision and Image Processing. With the labeling procedure, all
objects in a binary image are labeled with unique values, typically integer numbers. In the last few decades many novel proposals for CCL appeared, and only
some of them were compared on the same data and with the same implementation [3,11,14]. Therefore, the benchmarking framework Yet Another Connected
Components LAbeling Benchmark (YACCLAB in short) has been developed,
aiming to provide the fairest possible evaluation of CCL algorithms [10,15].

The performance evaluation task is not as easy as it may seem, as there
are several aspects that could influence an algorithm. However, since CCL is a
well-defined problem, admitting a unique solution, the key elements influencing
the "speed" of an algorithm can be reduced to: the data on which tests are
performed, the quality of the implementations, the hardware capabilities, and
last but not least, the code optimization provided by the compiler.

For these reasons, the YACCLAB benchmark is based on two fundamental traits which aim at guaranteeing the reproducibility of the claims made by
research papers:

(i) A public dataset of binary images that covers different application scenarios,
    ranging from text analysis to video surveillance.
(ii) A set of open-source C++ algorithms implementations, on which anyone can
    contribute to, with extensions or improvements.

© Springer Nature Switzerland AG 2019
B. Kerautret et al. (Eds.): RRPR 2018, LNCS 11455, pp. 89–93, 2019.
https://doi.org/10.1007/978-3-030-23987-9_7

The results obtained with YACCLAB may vary when the computer architecture or the compiler change, but being the code publicly available, anyone can test the provided algorithms on his own setting, choosing the one which suits his needs best, and verify any claim found in literature.

Following this line of work, in this paper we describe the algorithmic and implementation details of a recently developed CCL algorithm, "Connected Component Labeling on DRAGs" (Directed Rooted Acyclic Graphs) [7], focusing on its integration with YACCLAB and on the installation procedure. A detailed analysis of parameters influence on the result is also provided.

The source code of the aforementioned algorithm is located at [1], whereas the benchmarking suite can be found at [4].

2   How to Test DRAG with YACCLAB

To correctly install and run YACCLAB the following packages, libraries and utilities are required:

- CMake 3.0.0 or higher (https://cmake.org);
- OpenCV 3.0 or higher (http://opencv.org),
- Gnuplot (http://www.gnuplot.info);
- C++11 compiler.

The installation procedure requires the following steps:

- Clone the GitHub repository [4];
- Install the software using CMake, which should automatically find OpenCV path, whether correctly installed on your OS, download the YACCLAB dataset, and create a C++ project for the selected compiler;
- Set the configuration file config.yaml placed in the installation folder and select the desired tests;
- Open the project, compile and run it.

There are six different tests available: *correctness* tests are an initial validation of the algorithms; *average* tests run algorithms on every image of a dataset, reporting for each method the average run-time; *average_with_steps* separates the labeling time of each scan, and that required to allocate/deallocate data structures; *density* and *granularity* use synthetic images to evaluate the performance of different approaches in terms of scalability on the number of pixels, foreground density and pattern granularity; *memory* tests report an indication on the expected number of memory accesses required by an algorithm on a reference dataset.

YACCLAB stores average results in three different formats: a plain text file, histogram charts, either in color and in gray-scale, and a LaTeX table, which can be directly included in research papers. If an algorithm employs multiple scans, results will display time spent in each of them separately, producing a stacked histogram chart as output.

All the algorithms included in YACCLAB employ a base interface and implement the following virtual methods:

- `PerformLabeling`: includes the whole algorithm code and it is necessary to perform average, density, granularity and size tests;
- `PerformLabelingWithSteps`: implements the algorithm, dividing it in steps (*i.e.* `alloc`/`dealloc`, `first_scan` and `second_scan` for those which have two scans, or `all_scan` for the others) in order to evaluate every step separately;
- `PerformLabelingMem`: is an implementation of the algorithm that traces the number of memory accesses whenever they occur.

The Union-Find strategy is independent from the CCL one, therefore all CCL algorithms invoke a templated Union-Find implementation. YACCLAB is then able to compare each algorithm (but those for which the labels solver is built-in) with four different labels solving strategies: standard Union-Find (UF), Union-Find with Path Compression (UFPC) [21], Interleaved Rem's algorithm with splicing (RemSP) [12] and Three Table Array (TTA) [16]. This standardization reduces the code variability, allowing to separate the Union-Find data structures from the ones of CCL algorithms, and provides fairer comparisons without negatively impacting the execution time.

The *NULL labeling*, also referred as NULL, defines a lower bound limit for the execution time of CCL algorithms on a given machine and a reference dataset. As the name suggests, the NULL algorithm does not provide the correct connected components of an image, but only copies the pixels from the input image into the output one. This "algorithm" allows to identify the minimum time required for allocating the memory of the output image, reading the input image and writing the output one. In this way, all the algorithms can be compared in terms of how costly the additional operations required are.

3 Experiments Reproducibility

The DRAG algorithm was tested on an Intel Core i7-4770 CPU @ 3.40 GHz (4 × 32 KB L1 cache, 4 × 256 KB L2 cache, and 8 MB of L3 cache) with Linux OS and GCC 7.2.0 compiler enabling the -O3 and -m32 flags.

The impact of the labels solver on the overall performance is typically limited for most algorithms, so we only reported results obtained with the UFPC solver on the state-of-the-art algorithms.

The DRAG performance have been compared on six different datasets: a collection of histological images [13] with an average amount of 1.21 million pixels to analyze and 484 components to label (Medical), fingerprint images [20], collected by using low-cost optical sensors or synthetically generated, with an average of 809 components to label (Fingerprints), high resolution historical document images [6,8,9] with more than 15000 components and a low foreground density (XDOCS), a dataset for people detection [5], tracking, action analysis and trajectory analysis with very low foreground density and few components to identify (3DPeS), a selection of documents [2,18,19] collected and scanned using a wide variety of equipment over time with a resolution varying from 150 to 300 DPI (Tobacco800), and a large set of standard resolution natural images [17] taken from Flickr (MirFlickr).

In order to execute the same experiments reported in [7] the `perform`, `algo-rithms`, and `average_datasets` fields in the configuration file must be set as follows:

```
perform: {correctness: true, average: true, average_with_steps: false,
        density: false, granularity: false, memory: false}
algorithms: [SAUF_UFPC, BBDT_UFPC, DRAG_UFPC, CTB_UFPC, PRED_UFPC, CT,
        labeling_NULL]
average_datasets: ["mirflickr", "fingerprints", "xdocs", "tobacco800",
        "3dpes", "medical"]
```

Average tests were repeated 10 times (setting the `tests_number.average` in the configuration file), and for each image the minimum execution time was considered. The use of minimum is justified by the fact that, in theory, an algorithm on a specific environment will always require the same time to execute. This time was computable in exact way on non multitasking single core processors (8086, 80286). Nowadays, too many unpredictable things could occur in background, independently with respect to the specific algorithm. Anyway, an algorithm cannot use less than the required clock cycles, so the best way to get the "real" execution time is to use the minimum value over multiple runs. The probability of having a higher execution time is then equal for all algorithms. For that reason, taking the minimum is the only way to get reproducible results from one execution of the benchmark to another on the same environment.

4   Conclusion

This paper describes how to setup the YACCLAB project to reproduce the result reported in [7]. The processor model –and in particular the cache sizes–, the RAM speed and the background tasks will influence the execution time. Nevertheless, the algorithms relative performance should remain extremely similar. Changing the OS or the compiler is instead likely to heavily influence the outcome.

References

1. The DRAG Algorithm. https://github.com/prittt/YACCLAB/blob/master/include/labeling_bolelli_2018.h. Accessed 13 Mar 2019
2. Agam, G., Argamon, S., Frieder, O., Grossman, D., Lewis, D.: The Complex Document Image Processing (CDIP) Test Collection Project. Illinois Institute of Technology (2006)
3. Allegretti, S., Bolelli, F., Cancilla, M., Grana, C.: Optimizing GPU-based connected components labeling algorithms. In: Third IEEE International Conference on Image Processing, Applications and Systems (IPAS) (2018)
4. The YACCLAB Project. https://github.com/prittt/YACCLAB. Accessed 13 Mar 2019
5. Baltieri, D., Vezzani, R., Cucchiara, R.: 3DPeS: 3D people dataset for surveillance and forensics. In: Proceedings of the 2011 Joint ACM Workshop on Human Gesture and Behavior Understanding, pp. 59–64. ACM (2011)

6. Bolelli, F.: Indexing of historical document images: ad hoc dewarping technique for handwritten text. In: Grana, C., Baraldi, L. (eds.) IRCDL 2017. CCIS, vol. 733, pp. 45–55. Springer, Cham (2017). https://doi.org/10.1007/978-3-319-68130-6_4

7. Bolelli, F., Baraldi, L., Cancilla, M., Grana, C.: Connected components labeling on DRAGs. In: 24th International Conference on Pattern Recognition, August 2018

8. Bolelli, F., Borghi, G., Grana, C.: Historical handwritten text images word spotting through sliding window HOG features. In: Battiato, S., Gallo, G., Schettini, R., Stanco, F. (eds.) ICIAP 2017. LNCS, vol. 10484, pp. 729–738. Springer, Cham (2017). https://doi.org/10.1007/978-3-319-68560-1_65

9. Bolelli, F., Borghi, G., Grana, C.: XDOCS: an application to index historical documents. In: Serra, G., Tasso, C. (eds.) IRCDL 2018. CCIS, vol. 806, pp. 151–162. Springer, Cham (2018). https://doi.org/10.1007/978-3-319-73165-0_15

10. Bolelli, F., Cancilla, M., Baraldi, L., Grana, C.: J. Real-Time Image Proc. (2018). https://doi.org/10.1007/s11554-018-0756-1

11. Bolelli, F., Cancilla, M., Grana, C.: Two more strategies to speed up connected components labeling algorithms. In: Battiato, S., Gallo, G., Schettini, R., Stanco, F. (eds.) ICIAP 2017. LNCS, vol. 10485, pp. 48–58. Springer, Cham (2017). https://doi.org/10.1007/978-3-319-68548-9_5

12. Dijkstra, E.W.: A Discipline of Programming. Prentice-Hall, Englewood Cliffs (1976)

13. Dong, F., et al.: Computational pathology to discriminate benign from malignant intraductal proliferations of the breast. PloS ONE 9(12), e114885 (2014)

14. Grana, C., Baraldi, L., Bolelli, F.: Optimized connected components labeling with pixel prediction. In: Blanc-Talon, J., Distante, C., Philips, W., Popescu, D., Scheunders, P. (eds.) ACIVS 2016. LNCS, vol. 10016, pp. 431–440. Springer, Cham (2016). https://doi.org/10.1007/978-3-319-48680-2_38

15. Grana, C., Bolelli, F., Baraldi, L., Vezzani, R.: YACCLAB - yet another connected components labeling benchmark. In: 23rd International Conference on Pattern Recognition, pp. 3109–3114 (2016)

16. He, L., Chao, Y., Suzuki, K.: A linear-time two-scan labeling algorithm. In: International Conference on Image Processing, vol. 5, pp. 241–244 (2007)

17. Huiskes, M.J., Lew, M.S.: The MIR Flickr retrieval evaluation. In: MIR 2008: Proceedings of the 2008 ACM International Conference on Multimedia Information Retrieval. ACM, New York (2008)

18. Lewis, D., Agam, G., Argamon, S., Frieder, O., Grossman, D., Heard, J.: Building a test collection for complex document information processing. In: Proceedings of the 29th Annual International ACM SIGIR Conference on Research and Development in Information Retrieval, pp. 665–666. ACM (2006)

19. The Legacy Tobacco Document Library (LTDL). University of California, San Francisco (2007)

20. Maltoni, D., Maio, D., Jain, A., Prabhakar, S.: Handbook of Fingerprint Recognition. Springer, London (2009). https://doi.org/10.1007/978-1-84882-254-2

21. Wu, K., Otoo, E., Suzuki, K.: Two strategies to speed up connected component labeling algorithms. Technical report LBNL-59102, Lawrence Berkeley National Laboratory (2005)

MATLAB Implementation Details of a Scalable Spectral Clustering Algorithm with the Cosine Similarity

Guangliang Chen$^{(\boxtimes)}$

Department of Mathematics & Statistics, San José State University,
San José, CA 95192-0103, USA
guangliang.chen@sjsu.edu

Abstract. We present the implementation details of a scalable spectral clustering algorithm with cosine similarity (ICPR 2018, Beijing, China), which are based on simple, efficient matrix operations. The sensitivity of its parameters is also discussed.

1 Introduction

In our recent work [1] we introduced a scalable implementation of various spectral clustering algorithms, such as the Ng-Jordan-Weiss (NJW) algorithm [3], Normalized Cut (NCut) [4], and Diffusion Maps (DM) [2], in the special setting of cosine similarity by exploiting the product form of the weight matrix. We showed that if the data $\mathbf{X} \in \mathbb{R}^{n \times d}$ is large in size (n) but has some sort of low dimensional structure – either of low dimension (d) or being sparse (e.g. as a document-term matrix), then one can perform spectral clustering with cosine similarity solely based on three kinds of efficient operations on the data matrix: *elementwise manipulation*, *matrix-vector multiplication*, and *low-rank SVD*, before the final k-means step. As a result, the algorithm enjoys a linear complexity in the size of the data. We present the main steps of the algorithm in Algorithm 1 and refer the reader to the paper [1] for more details.

Remark 1. The outliers detected by the algorithm may be classified back to the main part of the data set by simple classifiers such as the nearest centroid classifier, or the k nearest neighbors (kNN) classifier.

2 Implementation Details

We implemented Algorithm 1 and conducted all the experiments in MATLAB. Note that the *Statistics and Machine Learning Toolbox* is needed because of the k-means function used in the final step (the rest of the steps consist of very basic linear algebra operations). If unavailable, the toolbox may be avoided if one uses a freely-available substitute k-means function such as *litekmeans*.[1]

---

[1] Available at http://www.cad.zju.edu.cn/home/dengcai/Data/Clustering.html.

© Springer Nature Switzerland AG 2019
B. Kerautret et al. (Eds.): RRPR 2018, LNCS 11455, pp. 94–97, 2019.
https://doi.org/10.1007/978-3-030-23987-9_8

Algorithm 1. Scalable Spectral Clustering with Cosine Similarity

---

Input: Data matrix $\mathbf{X} \in \mathbb{R}^{n \times d}$ (sparse or of moderate dimension, with L_2-normalized
   rows), #clusters k, clustering method (NJW, Ncut, or DM), fraction of outliers α

Output: Clusters $C_1, \ldots, C_k$ and a set of outliers C_0

1: Calculate the degree matrix $\mathbf{D} = \mathrm{diag}(\mathbf{X}(\mathbf{X}^T \mathbf{1}) - \mathbf{1})$ and remove the bottom
   $(100\alpha)\%$ of the input data that have the lowest degrees as outliers (stored in C_0).

2: For the remaining data, normalize them by $\widetilde{\mathbf{X}} = \mathbf{D}^{-1/2}\mathbf{X}$ and find its top k singular
   values $\lambda_1, \ldots, \lambda_k$ and corresponding left singular vectors $\widetilde{\mathbf{u}}_1, \ldots, \widetilde{\mathbf{u}}_k$ by rank-k SVD.
   Let $\boldsymbol{\Lambda} = \mathrm{diag}(\lambda_1, \ldots, \lambda_k) \in \mathbb{R}^{k \times k}$ and $\widehat{\mathbf{U}} = [\widetilde{\mathbf{u}}_1 \ldots \widetilde{\mathbf{u}}_k] \in \mathbb{R}^{n \times k}$.

3: Form the matrix $\mathbf{Y} \in \mathbb{R}^{n \times k}$ dependent on the clustering method (the rows of $\mathbf{Y}$
   are regarded as an embedding of the input data):

   – NJW: $\mathbf{Y} = \widetilde{\mathbf{U}}$;
   – NCut: $\mathbf{Y} = \mathbf{D}^{-1/2}\widetilde{\mathbf{U}}$
   – DM: $\mathbf{Y} = \mathbf{D}^{-1/2}\widetilde{\mathbf{U}}\boldsymbol{\Lambda}^t$, where t is a positive integer representing the number of
     diffusion steps.

4: Normalize the rows of $\mathbf{Y}$ to have unit ℓ_2 norm and apply the k-means algorithm
   to find k clusters $C_1, \ldots, C_k$.

To promote the simplicity and efficiency of the implementation, we did the
following things:

– We extended the value of the parameter t (hidden in DM) to include the
  other two clustering methods: NCut ($t = 0$) and NJW ($t = -1$).
– When the input data matrix $\mathbf{X}$ is sparse (e.g., as a document-term matrix),
  we take advantage of the sparse matrix operations in MATLAB.
– Diagonal matrices are always stored as vectors.
– All the multiplications between a matrix and a diagonal matrix (such as
  $\mathbf{D}^{-1/2}\mathbf{X}$ and $\mathbf{D}^{-1/2}\widetilde{\mathbf{U}}\boldsymbol{\Lambda}$), are implemented as element-wise binary operations
  through the *bsxfun* function in MATLAB. Additionally, the matrix-vector
  product $\mathbf{X}^T\mathbf{1}$ is implemented through *transpose(sum(X, 1))* in MATLAB.
– The *svds* function is used to find only the top k singular values and associated
  singular vectors of $\widetilde{\mathbf{X}}$.
– The k-means clustering is initialized with the default *plus* option, and uses
  10 restarts.
– We implemented the nearest centroid classifier for assigning the outliers back
  into the clusters due to its faster speed than k-NN.

The software, as well as the data sets used in [1] and this paper, has been
published at https://github.com/glsjsu/rprr2018.

3   Parameter Setting

The algorithm has only one parameter α that needs to be specified. It indicates the fraction of input data to be removed and treated as outliers.

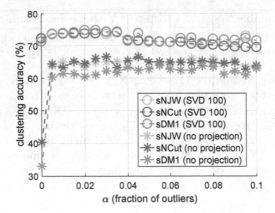

Fig. 1. Clustering accuracy rates of the three scalable methods on both versions of 20 newsgroups data corresponding to different α values.

Experiments conducted in [1] showed that the parameter α was not sensitive in the scalable NJW algorithm, as long as it is set bigger than zero.[2] Here, we further test the sensitivity of the α parameter in all three scalable methods on the same two versions of 20 newsgroups data [1] and report the accuracy results in Fig. 1.

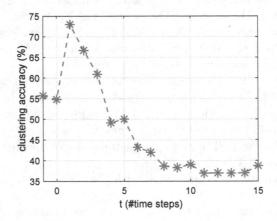

Fig. 2. Clustering accuracy of Algorithm 1 with DM and each value of $t = -1 : 15$ obtained on the top 30 categories of the TDT2 data set [1] ($\alpha = .01$ is always fixed). Note that the two special values $t = -1, 0$ correspond to the NJW and NCut options.

There is another parameter t in the code that needs to be specified, which in the case of DM represents the number of steps taken by a random walker.

---

[2] This is actually a necessary condition for the algorithm to work; see [1, Section III.B]. The value zero was included to verify the necessity of the condition.

In general, its optimal value is data-dependent. We have observed that DM with $t = 1$ often gives better accuracy than NCut (corresponding to $t = 0$); see Fig. 2 for an example.

4   Conclusions

We presented the MATLAB implementation details of a scalable spectral clustering algorithm with cosine similarity. The code consists of a few lines of simple linear algebra operations and is very efficient and fast. There are two parameters associated to the algorithm – α and t – but they are easy to tune: for the former, it is insensitive and we observed that the value $\alpha = .01$ often works adequately well; for the latter, it is truly a parameter when DM is used and in that case, setting it to $t = 1$ seems to achieve good accuracy in most cases. Lastly, all steps except the last step of k-means clustering in Algorithm 1 are deterministic and thus for fixed data and parameter values, the code yields very consistent results (any inconsistency is caused by the k-means clustering step).

Acknowledgments. We thank the anonymous reviewers for helpful feedback. G. Chen was supported by the Simons Foundation Collaboration Grant for Mathematicians.

References

1. Chen, G.: Scalable spectral clustering with cosine similarity. In: Proceedings of the 24th International Conference on Pattern Recognition (ICPR), Beijing, China, pp. 314–319 (2018)
2. Coifman, R., Lafon, S.: Diffusion maps. Appl. Comput. Harmon. Anal. **21**(1), 5–30 (2006)
3. Ng, A., Jordan, M., Weiss, Y.: On spectral clustering: analysis and an algorithm. Adv. Neural Inf. Process. Syst. **14**, 849–856 (2001)
4. Shi, J., Malik, J.: Normalized cuts and image segmentation. IEEE Trans. Pattern Anal. Mach. Intell. **22**(8), 888–905 (2000)

On the Implementation of ALFA – Agglomerative Late Fusion Algorithm for Object Detection

Iuliia Saveleva[✉] [iD] and Evgenii Razinkov[iD]

Institute of Computational Mathematics and Information Technologies,
Kazan Federal University, Kazan, Russia
Ju0Saveleva@stud.kpfu.ru, Evgenij.Razinkov@kpfu.ru

Abstract. The paper focuses on implementation details of ALFA – an agglomerative late fusion algorithm for object detection. ALFA agglomeratively clusters detector predictions while taking into account bounding box locations and class scores. We discuss the source code of ALFA and another late fusion algorithm – Dynamic Belief Fusion (DBF). The workflow and the hyperparameters necessary to reproduce the published results are presented. We also provide a framework for evaluation of late fusion algorithms like ALFA, DBF and Non-Maximum Suppression with arbitrary object detectors.

Keywords: Object detection · Late fusion · Agglomerative clustering

1 Introduction

Object detection is an important and challenging computer vision problem. State of the art object detectors, such as Faster R-CNN, YOLO, SSD and DeNet, rely on deep convolutional neural networks and show remarkable results in terms of accuracy and speed. Fusing results of several object detection methods is a common way to increase accuracy of object detection. In the companion paper [1] a new late fusion algorithm for object detection called ALFA was proposed. ALFA relies on agglomerative clustering and shows state of the art results on PASCAL VOC 2007 and 2012 object detection datasets.

We also implemented Dynamic Belief Fusion – state of the art late fusion algorithm for object detection proposed in [2] – as our baseline, since the implementation from authors is not available.

Here we describe our implementation of ALFA and DBF providing pseudocode for the key functions of these methods. We also provide hyperparameter values required to reproduce results from [1] on PASCAL VOC 2012 dataset. Results on PASCAL VOC 2007 are not reproducible due to randomness of a cross-validation procedure.

Link to our implementation: http://github.com/IuliiaSaveleva/ALFA. All the details required to successfully run the code are provided in README.md.

© Springer Nature Switzerland AG 2019
B. Kerautret et al. (Eds.): RRPR 2018, LNCS 11455, pp. 98–103, 2019.
https://doi.org/10.1007/978-3-030-23987-9_9

2   Implementation

Assume object detection task for K classes and N trained object detectors $D_1, D_2, ..., D_N$. Given an image I object detector produces a set of predictions:

$$D_i(I) = \{p_1, ..., p_{m_i}\}, \quad p = (r, c),$$

where m_i is the number of detected objects, r represents four coordinates of the axis-aligned bounding box and c is class scores tuple of size $(K + 1)$, including "no object" score $c^{(0)}$.

2.1   ALFA Implementation

The steps of ALFA are given below.

2.1.1   Agglomerative Clustering of Base Detectors Predictions

We assume that prediction bounding box r_i and class scores c_i should be similar to other prediction bounding box r_j and class scores c_j if they correspond to the same object. Let C_i and C_j be two clusters and $\sigma(p, \tilde{p})$ – similarity score function between predictions p and $\tilde{p}$. We define the following similarity score function with hyperparameter τ for prediction clusters:

$$\sigma(C_i, C_j) = \min_{p \in C_i, \tilde{p} \in C_j} \sigma(p, \tilde{p}), \quad \text{while} \quad max_{i,j} \sigma(C_i, C_j) \geq \tau. \tag{1}$$

We propose the following measure of similarity between predictions:

$$\sigma(p_i, p_j) = IoU(r_i, r_j)^\gamma \cdot BC(\bar{c}_i, \bar{c}_j)^{1-\gamma}, \tag{2}$$

where $\gamma \in [0, 1]$ is a hyperparameter, BC – Bhattacharyya coefficient as a measure of similarity between class scores ($\bar{c}$ is obtained from class score tuple c by omitting the zeroth *"no object"* component and renormalizing):

$$BC(\bar{c}_i, \bar{c}_j) = \sum_{k=1}^{K} \sqrt{\bar{c}_i^{(k)} \bar{c}_j^{(k)}}, \quad \bar{c}^{(k)} = \frac{c^{(k)}}{1 - c^{(0)}}, \quad k = 1, ...K, \tag{3}$$

IoU – intersection over union coefficient which is widely used as a measure of similarity between bounding boxes:

$$IoU(r_i, r_j) = \frac{r_i \cap r_j}{r_i \cup r_j}. \tag{4}$$

See Algorithm 1.

2.1.2 Class Scores Aggregation

Assume that predictions from detectors $D_{i_1}, D_{i_2}, ..., D_{i_s}$ were assigned to object proposal π. We assign an additional low-confidence class scores tuple to this object proposal for every detector that missed:

$$c_{lc} = \left(1 - \varepsilon, \frac{\varepsilon}{K}, \frac{\varepsilon}{K}, ..., \frac{\varepsilon}{K}\right), \tag{5}$$

where ε is a hyperparameter.

Each method uses one of two class scores aggregation strategies:

– *Averaging fusion*:

$$c_{\pi}^{(k)} = \frac{1}{N}\left(\sum_{d=1}^{s} c_{i_d}^{(k)} + (N - s) \cdot c_{lc}^{(k)}\right), k = 0, ..., K. \tag{6}$$

– *Multiplication fusion*:

$$c_{\pi}^{(k)} = \frac{\tilde{c}_{\pi}^{(k)}}{\sum_i \tilde{c}_{\pi}^{(i)}}, \quad \tilde{c}_{\pi}^{(k)} = \left(c_{lc}^{(k)}\right)^{N-s} \prod_{d=1}^{s} c_{i_d}^{(k)}, \quad k = 0, ..., K. \tag{7}$$

2.1.3 Bounding Box Aggregation

All methods have the same bounding box aggregation strategy:

$$r_{\pi} = \frac{1}{\sum_{i \in \pi} c_i^{(l)}} \sum_{i \in \pi} c_i^{(l)} \cdot r_i, \quad \text{where} \quad l = \underset{k \geq 1}{\operatorname{argmax}} \, c_{\pi}^{(k)}. \tag{8}$$

Best ALFA parameters are provided in Table 1:

Table 1. Best ALFA parameters.

Detectors	Methods	Confidence threshold	mAP	τ	γ	Scores aggregation strategy	ε	δ
SSD + DeNet	Fast ALFA	0.05	mAP	0.73	0.25	Averaging	0.26	True
	ALFA	0.015						
	Fast ALFA	0.05	mAP-s	0.48	0.22	Multiplication	0.56	True
	ALFA	0.015						
SSD + DeNet + Faster R-CNN	Fast ALFA	0.05	mAP	0.74	0.3	Averaging	0.39	False
	ALFA	0.015						
	Fast ALFA	0.05	mAP-s	0.75	0.28	Multiplication	0.17	True
	ALFA	0.015						

Algorithm 1. Agglomerative Clustering

Data: $D = D_1(I) \cup ... \cup D_N(I)$; Hyperparameters: γ, $\tau \in [0,1]$,
   $\delta = \{False, True\}$

begin

   Set $\sigma(p_i, p_j) = IoU(r_i, r_j)^\gamma \cdot BC(\bar{c}_i, \bar{c}_j)^{1-\gamma}$

   $G = \{g_{ij}\}$, $g_{ij} = 1$ **if** $((label_i = label_j)$ or $\delta = False)$, 0 **otherwise**

   $U = \{u_{ij}\}$, $u_{ij} = 1$ **if** $\nexists t : p_i, p_j \in D_t(I)$, 0 **otherwise**

   $S = \{s_{ij}\}$, $s_{ij} = \sigma(p_i, p_j)$ **if** $\sigma(p_i, p_j) > \tau$ **else** 0

   $Q = G \circ U \circ S$

   $k = 0$; $W_0 = Sign(Q)$

   do

      $k = k + 1$

      $W_k = Sign(W_{k-1} \cdot W_{k-1})$

   while $W_k \neq W_{k-1}$;

   $M = UniqueRows(W_k)$

   for $i := 1$ **to** $|M|$ **do**

      $Clusters_i = \{C_j = \{p_j\}|m_{ij} = 1\}$

      do

         $sim = \max\limits_{C,C'} \min\limits_{p \in C, p' \in C'} \sigma(p, p')$, $C, C' \in Clusters_i$

         if $sim > \tau$ **then**

            $C_i = C_i \cup C_j$

            $Clusters_i = Clusters_i \setminus C_j$

      while $sim > \tau$;

return $\cup_i Clusters_i$

2.2 DBF Implementation

Our implementation of DBF consists of the following steps:

1. Compute PR-curves PR_i^k for each class k and each detector D_i, $i = 1, ..., N$;
2. Construct detection vectors for each $p \in D_i(I)$, $i = 1, ..., N$, and calculation of basic probabilities of hypothesis according to label l and PR_i^k. See Algorithm 2;
3. Join basic probabilities by Dempster-Shaffer combination rule:

$$m_f(A) = \frac{1}{N} \sum_{X_1 \cap X_2 ... \cap X_K = A} \prod_{i=1}^{K} m_i(X_i),$$

where $N = \sum_{X_1 \cap X_2 ... \cap X_K \neq \varnothing} \prod_{i=1}^{K} m_i(X_i)$, to determine fused basic probabilities $m_f(T)$ and $m_f(\neg T)$;
4. Get fused score as $\bar{s} = m_f(T) - m_f(\neg T)$;
5. Apply NMS to bounding boxes r and scores $\bar{s}$. In order to help DBF more on NMS step we sort detections by score $\bar{s}$ and precision from PR_i^k, $k = l$, if detections had equal $\bar{s}$ values.

Algorithm 2. DBF algorithm: Constructing detection vectors and calculating basic probabilities of hypothesis

---

Data: $p = (r, c)$, $D_i(I)$, $i = 1, ..., N$, PR^k; Hyperparameter: n
begin

    for $i := 1$ **to** N **do**

        if $p \notin D_i(I)$ **then**

            Find $\bar{p}_i = (\bar{r}_i, \bar{c}_i)$ that $l = l_i$ and $max(IoU(r, r_i))$,
            $l = \text{argmax}_{k \geq 1} c^k$

            if $IoU(r, \bar{r}_i) > 0.5$ **then**

                | $d_i = \bar{c}_i^{\bar{l}_i}$

            else

                $d_i = -\infty$

        else

            $d_i = c^l$

    Calculate $\{m(T), m(\neg T), m(I)\}$ for each component of detection vectors d:

    for $i := 1$ **to** N **do**

        Get precision p and recall r from PR^k, $k = \text{argmax}_{k \geq 1} c^k$, using score from d_i

        $m(T)_i = p$

        $p_{bpd} = 1 - r^n$ – precision of best possible detector

        $m(\neg T)_i = 1 - p_{bpd}$

        $m(I)_i = p_{bpd} - p$

return $m(T)$, $m(\neg T)$, $m(I)$

Best DBF parameters are provided in Table 2:

Table 2. Best DBF parameters.

	SSD + DeNet		SSD + DeNet + Faster R-CNN	
	mAP	mAP-s	mAP	mAP-s
n	16	16	18	14
Confidence threshold	0.015			

3 Conclusion

This paper had presented implementation details of ALFA and DBF late fusion methods for object detection. We provide source code and hyperparameter values that allow one to reproduce results from [1] on PASCAL VOC 2012.

Acknowledgment. I. Saveleva was funded by the Russian Government support of the Program of Competitive Growth of Kazan Federal University among World's Leading Academic Centers and by Russian Foundation of Basic Research, project number 16-01-00109a.

References

1. Razinkov, E., Saveleva, I., Matas, J.: ALFA: agglomerative late fusion algorithm for object detection. In: 2018 24th International Conference on Pattern Recognition (ICPR), pp. 2594–2599. IEEE, August 2018
2. Lee, H., Kwon, H., Robinson, R., Nothwang, W., Marathe, A.: Dynamic belief fusion for object detection. In: 2016 IEEE Winter Conference on Applications of Computer Vision (WACV), pp. 1–9. IEEE (2016)

On Reproducibility of Deep Convolutional Neural Networks Approaches

Gabriele Piantadosi[✉], Stefano Marrone, and Carlo Sansone

DIETI - University of Naples Federico II, Naples, Italy
{gabriele.piantadosi,stefano.marrone,carlo.sansone}@unina.it

Abstract. Nowadays, Machine Learning techniques are more and more pervasive in several application fields. In order to perform an evaluation as reliable as possible, it is necessary to consider the reproducibility of these models both at training and inference time. With the introduction of Deep Learning (DL), the assessment of reproducibility became a critical issue due to heuristic considerations made at training time that, although improving the optimization performances of such complex models, can result in non-deterministic outcomes and, therefore, not reproducible models. The aim of this paper is to quantitatively highlight the reproducibility problem of DL approaches, proposing to overcome it by using statistical considerations. We show that, even if the models generated by using several times the same data show differences in the inference phase, the obtained results are not statistically different. In particular, this short paper analyzes, as a case study, our ICPR2018 DL based approach for the breast segmentation in DCE-MRI, demonstrating the reproducibility of the reported results.

1 Introduction

With the spread of Machine Learning techniques in several application fields, performing a reliable evaluation of obtained results requires to consider their reproducibility both at training and inference time. This is a non-trivial problem for Deep Learning (DL) based applications, since their training and optimization strongly relies on stochastic procedures, thus undermining the basis for results reproducibility. Although these considerations can improve performances, they can result in non-deterministic outcomes and, therefore, not reproducible models. This problem is usually faced by using probabilistic considerations that, however, do not really fit some application field standard (as medical imaging analysis with Computer-Aided Detection and Diagnosis systems - CAD [4]) that requires demonstrable proofs of effectiveness and repeatability of results. Our opinion is that in those cases it is very important to clarify if and to what extent a DL based application is stable and repeatable over than effective.

Therefore, the aim of this paper is to quantitatively highlight the reproducibility problem of Convolutional Neural Networks (CNN) based approaches, proposing to overcome it by using statistical considerations. As a case of study,

B. Kerautret et al. (Eds.): RRPR 2018, LNCS 11455, pp. 104–109, 2019.
https://doi.org/10.1007/978-3-030-23987-9_10

we analyze our ICPR2018 [5] proposal for the breast tissues segmentation in DCE-MRI by using a modified version of a 2D U-Net CNN [6], a very effective deep architecture for semantic segmentation. The rest of the paper is organized as follows: Sect. 2 introduce the reproducibility issue for the deep learning frameworks; Sect. 3 describes the proposed validation procedure, briefly introducing the considered breast segmentation problem; Sect. 4 reports reproducibility results, while Sect. 5 draws some conclusions.

2 Reproducibility of Deep Learning Models

Convolution GP-GPU library (i.e. cuDNN from NVidia) default configuration exploits stochastic and speculative procedures that, although increase the execution speed, introduce uncontrollable factors that can result in not reproducible outcomes. In particular, the following cuDNN routines do not guarantee the reproducibility because they use atomic operations to speed up the computation: *cudnnConvolutionBackwardFilter*, *cudnnConvolutionBackwardData*, *cudnnPoolingBackward* and *cudnnSpatialTfSamplerBackward* [1]. In all the frameworks using cuDNN (such as Tensorflow), this causes non-deterministic gradient updates, mainly due to underlying non-deterministic reductions for convolutions (i.e. floating point operations are not necessarily associative) leading to randomness in the trained models.

Thus, in this paper, we propose to shift the reproducibility issue from a strictly combinatorial problem to a statistical one, in order to validate the model robustness and stability more than its perfect outcomes predictability that, in our experiments, can strongly vary across different frameworks and hardware used. To this aim, we performed a Montecarlo-like repetition experimentation, considering the model stable, and thus repeatable, if results stay within a given confidence interval.

3 Case Study: Whole Breast Segmentation via CNNs

In our ICPR2018 [5] paper we propose to perform the breast tissues segmentation by considering the 3D volume as a composition of 2D sagittal slices and using a modified 2D U-Net (Fig. 1): (a) the output feature-map was set to one to speed up the convergence; (b) zero-padding, with a size-preserving strategy, was applied for preserving the output shapes; (c) batch normalization (BN) layers was inserted after each convolution. The network was trained by minimizing the task-specific *loss*: $1 - DSC$. Where DSC is the Dice Similarity Coefficient defined in Eq. 1, $n(\cdot)$ represents the enclosed volume number of voxels, GS represents the gold standard and SEG represents the segmented volume.

$$DSC = (2 \cdot n(GS \cap SEG))/(n(GS) + n(SEG)) \tag{1}$$

The network kernel weights have been initialized from a standard distribution $\mathcal{N}(0, \sqrt{2/(\text{fan\_in} + \text{fan\_out})})$ [2], where fan_in and fan_out are respectively the

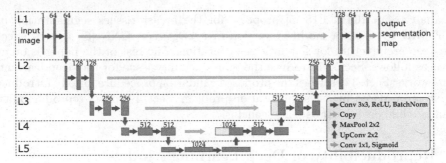

Fig. 1. Our U-Net proposal for the breast tissues segmentation. The left side performs the contracting path while the right side performs the expansive path

convolution layer input and output features sizes, while the bias weights have been initialized to a constant value of 0.1 to avoid slow-start learning when using ReLu activation functions.

ADAM optimizer [3] was used to minimize the loss function setting $\beta_1 = 0.9$, $\beta_2 = 0.999$ and learning_rate $= 0.001$, with an inverse time decay strategy. Performances were evaluated on 42 subjects DCE-MRI data acquired using a $1.5T$ scanner (Magnetom Symphony, Siemens) equipped with breast coil, considering only the pre-contrast series.

The proposed CNNs have been implemented using the Keras high-level neural networks API in Python 3.6 with the TensorFlow (v1.9) as back-end. With the aim of also consider the likely impact of the underlying GPU family, the Python scripts have been evaluated on the following configurations:

Conf. 'A' A virtual environment freely offered by Google Colaboratory[1]. The virtual machine has an Intel(R) Xeon(R) @ 2.2 GHz CPU (2 cores), 13 GB RAM and an Nvidia K80 GPU (Tesla family) with 12 GB GRAM.

Conf. 'B' A physical server hosted in our university HPC center[2] equipped with 2 x Intel(R) Xeon(R) Intel(R) 2.13 GHz CPUs (4 cores), 32 GB RAM and an Nvidia Titan Xp GPU (Pascal family) with 12 GB GRAM.

The assessment was performed by using a patient-based 10-fold Cross Validation (CV), in order to prevent slices from the same subject belonging to two different folds, applying a training/test data standardization using the median and standard deviation calculated only on the training patients' fold. To validate the repeatability of our model, we repeated the execution 50 times. We used the same initialization seeds for the random numbers generators to try highlighting only the uncertainty due to random considerations introduced by the optimization tools' randomness. The obtained breast-mask is compared to the gold standard in terms of Dice Similarity Coefficient (DSC) index.

---

[1] https://colab.research.google.com.
[2] http://www.scope.unina.it.

4   Results

For brevity reasons, this section reports only the first 10 executions of the Montecarlo analysis. Each Montecarlo execution applies a 10-fold cross-validation producing 10 folds containing the 42 patient segmentations[3]. The median values of a part of the Montecarlo execution are reported in the Tables 1 and 2.

Table 1. Results obtained for each of the first 10 out of 50 Montecarlo executions of the 10-fold cross-validation for our approach, using the conf. 'A'. The results presented in ICPR2018 are also reported in bold. Median values with corresponding 95% confidence intervals (LB: LowerBound, UB: UpperBound) are reported.

Repetition	DSC [%]	LB [%]	UB [%]
ICPR2018 [5]	95.90	95.16	96.64
Rep.01	95.80	95.24	96.37
Rep.02	96.19	95.62	96.75
Rep.03	95.85	95.38	96.39
Rep.04	96.11	95.69	96.57
Rep.05	96.04	95.15	96.62
Rep.06	95.90	95.02	96.60
Rep.07	96.25	95.29	96.52
Rep.08	95.93	95.44	96.56
Rep.09	95.95	95.38	96.36
Rep.10	95.89	95.35	96.43

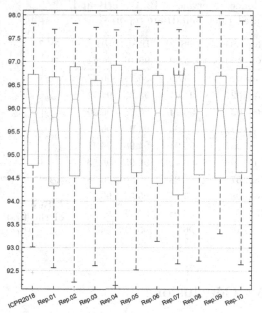

Fig. 2. Boxplots of the ICPR2018 results and of the first 10 out of 50 Montecarlo executions, using the conf. 'A'. Statistics are in Table 1

Both Tables 1 and 2 show how the computational frameworks for the optimization of deep learning models suffer from reproducibility during the training phase producing different models and thus, different results. This problem is not limited to the analyzed framework, Tensorflow, neither in the used GPU architecture, but lies in the Nvidia libraries as discussed in Sect. 2. Nevertheless, the randomness introduced in the trained models (by fixing the seeds of all the random numbers generators) produces not statistically different results as graphically shown in the Fig. 2.

---

[3] Scripts where available to reviewers for reproducing the executions.

Table 2. Results obtained for each of the first 10 out of 50 Montecarlo executions of the 10-fold cross-validation for our approach, using the conf. 'B'. The results presented in ICPR2018 are also reported in bold. Median values with corresponding 95% confidence intervals (LB: LowerBound, UB: UpperBound) are reported.

Repetition	DSC [%]	LB [%]	UB [%]
ICPR2018 [5]	95.90	95.16	96.64
Rep.01	95.89	95.18	96.47
Rep.02	95.91	95.25	96.32
Rep.03	96.14	95.08	96.66
Rep.04	95.90	94.92	96.48
Rep.05	96.01	94.98	96.41
Rep.06	96.12	94.95	96.53
Rep.07	96.03	95.56	96.28
Rep.08	95.95	95.52	96.29
Rep.09	96.08	94.77	96.39
Rep.10	96.12	95.31	96.48

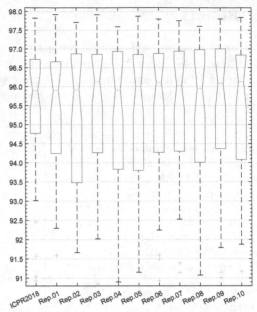

Fig. 3. Boxplots of the ICPR2018 results and of the first 10 out of 50 Montecarlo executions, using the conf. 'B'. Statistics are in Table 2

5 Conclusions

The aim of this paper was to quantitatively highlight the problem of the reproducibility of Deep Learning approaches, proposing to overcome it by using statistical considerations. We quantitatively highlighted, in Table 1, the reproducibility problem of Convolutional Neural Networks (CNN) based approaches evaluating our DL approach for breast segmentation proposed in [5]). *It is worth noting that this problem is not limited to the analyzed framework, Tensorflow, neither in the used GPU architecture, but lies in the Nvidia libraries as discussed in* Sect. 2. Analyzing the boxplots in Figs. 2 and 3, we can state that our CNN-based model is stable to the different training executions over different hardware configurations, since the confidence intervals obtained on the tests data overlap. We have been able to demonstrate that the reproducibility issue can be shifted from a strictly combinatorial problem to a statistical one, in order to validate the model robustness and stability more than its perfect outcomes predictability. Generally speaking, the randomness introduced with the advent of optimization engines for deep learning models, even if it may impact on the results of a reliable and reproducible research, only shift the attention on the statistical validity of the obtained outcomes. In fact, a model showing large variations in results will have very wide confidence intervals leading to unreliable results.

Acknowledgments. The authors gratefully acknowledge the support of NVIDIA Corporation with the donation of the Titan Xp GPU used for this research, the availability of the Calculation Centre SCoPE of the University of Naples Federico II and thank the SCoPE academic staff for the given support. The authors are also grateful to Dr. Antonella Petrillo, Head of Division of Radiology and PhD Roberta Fusco, Department of Diagnostic Imaging, Radiant and Metabolic Therapy, "Istituto Nazionale dei Tumori Fondazione G. Pascale" - IRCCS, Naples, Italy, for providing data. This work is part of the "BLADE: Breast Lesions Analysis by DEep learning approaches" project.

References

1. Nvidia deep learning sdk: cudnn developer guide. https://docs.nvidia.com/deeplearning/sdk/cudnn-developer-guide/index.html#reproducibility. Accessed 05 Aug 2018
2. Glorot, X., Bengio, Y.: Understanding the difficulty of training deep feedforward neural networks. In: Proceedings of the Thirteenth International Conference on Artificial Intelligence and Statistics, pp. 249–256 (2010)
3. Kingma, D., Ba, J.: Adam: a method for stochastic optimization. arXiv preprint arXiv:1412.6980 (2014)
4. Piantadosi, G., Marrone, S., Fusco, R., Sansone, M., Sansone, C.: A comprehensive computer-aided diagnosis for breast T1w DCE-MRI via quantitative dynamical features and spatio-temporal local binary patterns. IET Comput. Vis. (2018)
5. Piantadosi, G., Sansone, M., Sansone, C.: Breast segmentation in MRI via U-net deep convolutional neural networks. In: 24rd International Conference on Pattern Recognition (ICPR) (2018)
6. Ronneberger, O., Fischer, P., Brox, T.: U-Net: convolutional networks for biomedical image segmentation. In: Navab, N., Hornegger, J., Wells, W.M., Frangi, A.F. (eds.) MICCAI 2015. LNCS, vol. 9351, pp. 234–241. Springer, Cham (2015). https://doi.org/10.1007/978-3-319-24574-4_28

Some Comments on Variational Bayes Block Sparse Modeling with Correlated Entries

Shruti Sharma$^{(\boxtimes)}$ ⓘ, Santanu Chaudhury$^{(\boxtimes)}$, and Jayadeva$^{(\boxtimes)}$

Indian Institute of Technology Delhi, New Delhi, India
shruti_sml@yahoo.com, {santanuc,jayadeva}@ee.iitd.ac.in

Abstract. We present some details of Bayesian block sparse modeling using hierarchical prior having deterministic and random parameters when entries within the blocks are correlated. In particular, the effect of the threshold to prune out variance parameters of algorithms corresponding to several choices of marginals, viz. multivariate Jeffery prior, multivariate Laplace distribution and multivariate Student's t distribution, is discussed. We also provide details of experiments with Electroencephalograph (EEG) data which shed some light on the possible applicability of the proposed Sparse Variational Bayes framework.

Keywords: Bayesian block sparse modeling ·
Gaussian Mixture Model (GSM) · Sparse Variational Bayes (SVB) ·
Electroencephalograph (EEG) data

1 Introduction to Sparse Variational Bayes Framework

Compressed Sensing problem aims at solving an undetermined system of linear equations:

$$\mathbf{y} = \Phi\mathbf{x} + \mathbf{v} \tag{1}$$

where $\mathbf{y} \in \mathbb{R}^{m \times 1}$ is the observation vector, $\mathbf{x} \in \mathbb{R}^{n \times 1}$ is the unknown solution vector with $n >> m$, $\mathbf{v}$ is the unknown noise vector and $\Phi \in \mathbb{R}^{m \times n}$ is the known *random* matrix with full row rank and satisfies *Restricted Isometry Property*. Infinitely many $\mathbf{x}$ can solve (1) provided solution exists and thus we need to make some assumptions to make the problem well defined [1]. Sparsity is one of the viable assumption which has received a lot of attention in the recent times. In addition to sparsity, sometimes signals exhibit additional structures in the form of blocks and we have block linear sparse model [2]:

$$\mathbf{y} = \sum_{i=1}^{g} \Phi^i \mathbf{x}_i + \mathbf{v} \tag{2}$$

Supported by grant NPPE-II (RP02874) as per letter no. DEITY/R&D/TDC/13(2)/ 2013 of Ministry of Communications and Information Technology, India.

© Springer Nature Switzerland AG 2019
B. Kerautret et al. (Eds.): RRPR 2018, LNCS 11455, pp. 110–117, 2019.
https://doi.org/10.1007/978-3-030-23987-9_11

where $\Phi^i \in \mathbb{R}^{m \times d_i}$, $\mathbf{x}_i \in \mathbb{R}^{d_i \times 1}$ and $\sum_{i=1}^{g} d_i = n$, g being the number of non-zero blocks and d_i being the size of ith block.

Generalized Sparse Variational Bayes (cSVB) framework is a three level hierarchical estimation framework [3] which is extension of the work proposed in [4,5] for block sparse signals with correlated entries. At first level, it assigns heavy tailed sparsity promoting priors (which can also be expressed as Gaussian Scale Mixtures with appropriate mixing density [6]) over each block:

$$\mathbf{x}_i = \frac{1}{\sqrt{\alpha_i}} \mathbf{C}_i \mathbf{g} \qquad \forall i = 1, \ldots, g \tag{3}$$

where $\mathbf{g} \sim \mathcal{N}(\mathbf{0}_{d_i}, \mathbf{I}_{d_i})$, α_i is the inverse variance random parameter and $\mathbf{B}_i^{-1} \triangleq \mathbf{C}_i \mathbf{C}_i^t \in \mathbb{R}^{d_i \times d_i}$ is the covariance deterministic parameter matrix of the block $\mathbf{x}_i$. At second level, depending on the choice of prior distribution over parameters α_i, various heavy tailed distributions can be induced over $\mathbf{x}_i$ viz. multivariate Laplace distribution, multivariate Student's t distribution and multivariate Jeffery's prior. At third level, we impose different priors over hyperparameters. Graphical model representing this framework is shown in Fig. 1.

In this framework, α_is play an important role in inducing sparsity in the solution vector. When $\alpha_i = \infty$, the corresponding ith block of $\mathbf{x}$ becomes 0. Due to the mechanism of Automatic Relevance Determination (ARD), most of the α_i tend to infinity and thus block sparsity is encouraged. However, in the presence of noise, α_i never becomes ∞ and thus a threshold is used to prune out large α_i. This work aims at addressing the effect of threshold to prune out α_i parameters (Sect. 2) in terms of mean square error, failure rate and speed of the algorithms proposed[1] in our work [3]. For notations and other details, please refer [3]. We also demonstrate the utility of the framework for EEG data reconstruction problem [7] and Steady-State Visual Evoked Potential EEG recognition problem [8,9].

2   Effect of Threshold to Prune Out Variance Parameters

We randomly generated the unknown solution vector $\mathbf{x}$ of length $n = 480$ with total non-zero coefficients being 24, occurring in blocks at random locations. Coefficients within each blocks were generated as AR(1) process with common AR coefficient ρ. $m = 50$ was kept fixed and block size was varied from 1 to 6. $\Phi \in \mathbb{R}^{m \times n}$ consisted of columns drawn from a standard Gaussian distribution with unit ℓ_2 norm. Zero mean $\mathbf{v}$ was added to measurements $\mathbf{y} = \Phi\mathbf{x} + \mathbf{v}$ with variance depending on the desired SNR. For analysis of algorithms, we carried out simple experiments over synthetic data of 200 independent trials with different realizations of measurement matrix Φ and true signal $\mathbf{x}$. Correlation coefficient ρ was kept 0.8. We investigated the effect of threshold value to prune out α_i and considered threshold values: 10, 50, 100, 10^3, 10^4, 10^5, 10^6, 10^7, 10^8.

---

[1] The codes for [3] can be found at https://github.com/shruti51/cSVB.

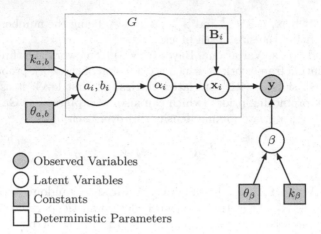

Fig. 1. Graphical Model representing the Bayesian Model. Red plate (the box labeled G) represents G nodes of which only a single node ($\mathbf{x}_i$ and related variables) is shown explicitly (Color figure online)

We measured the algorithm's performance in terms of failure rate (please refer [3] for definition of failure rate), MSE and speed.

From Figs. 2, 3 and 4, we see that α-pruning threshold plays an important role in determining the performance of the algorithms. Figure 2 shows that while optimal performance, in terms of failure rate, of BSBL variants and SVB variants depends on the threshold, cSVB variants do not depend much on α-pruning threshold. This is desirable in the sense that we don't want our algorithms to depend much on the parameters of framework. It also shows that cSVB variants have outperformed SVB variants and BSBL-BO. Figure 3 shows that SVB variants have again performed poorly but now BSBL-BO performance is comparable to that of cSVB variants. Finally, we see from Fig. 4 that good performance of cSVB variants has come at a price of their computational complexity where time taken by cSVB variants is high as compared to BSBL-BO. SVB variants offer low complex algorithms as compared to cSVB and BSBL-BO which do not involve extra computational burden of inversion of matrix $\mathbf{B}$ and thus attributing to their fast execution speed at low threshold values.

To summarize, we say that cSVB variants have a potential to recover block sparse signals with high fidelity irrespective of the α_i-pruning threshold. But this comes at a cost of high computational time.

3   Experiments with EEG Data

3.1   Reconstruction Performance of Algorithms with EEG Signals

We have used eeglab_data.set from EEGLAB which has 32 channels. Dataset and related MATLAB codes were downloaded from [10]. Each channel consists

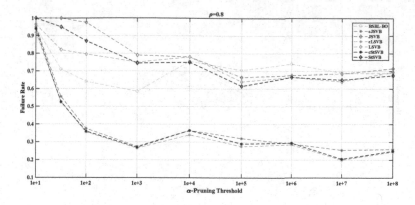

Fig. 2. Failure rate versus α-pruning threshold

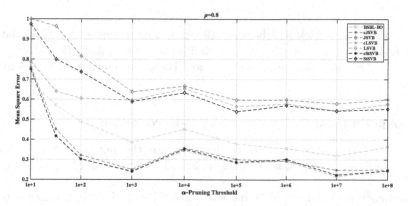

Fig. 3. Mean square error versus α-pruning threshold

of 80 epochs with 384 samples in every channel and epoch was processed independently. The data matrix was firstly transformed using Discrete Cosine Transform (DCT) and sensing matrix Φ was considered to be binary matrix of dimensions 150×384, each column of which contained 10 ones and rest zeros [7]. This model can be written as:

$$\mathbf{y} = \Phi\mathbf{x} = \Phi\mathbf{D}\mathbf{z} \tag{4}$$

where $\mathbf{y}$ are compressed measurements, $\mathbf{x}$ are original measurements and $\mathbf{z} = \mathbf{D}^{-1}\mathbf{x}$ are DCT coefficients and have few significant entries due to 'energy compaction' property of the transform. Block partitioning was kept equal and block size 24.

The reconstruction performance of all the algorithms is shown in Fig. 5. Due to our inability to interpret EEG signals, it is very difficult to assess the quality of EEG reconstruction by the proposed algorithm. However, it can be seen that at least all the algorithms have managed to capture the trends of original EEG signal. So, in this case, experiments suggest that EEG data does not exhibit

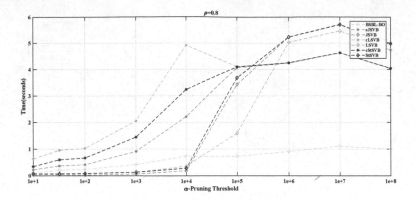

Fig. 4. Time (in seconds) versus α-pruning threshold

strong correlation which is otherwise also true in the sense that EEG data is highly non-stationary data. So, SVB variants can be seen as equally strong candidates for the analysis which do not model any correlation structure of the signal.

3.2   Experimental Results on SSVEP-Recognition

Main aim of this experiment is to demonstrate the power of Sparse Variational Bayesian framework in recognizing Steady-State Visual Evoked Potential (SSVEP).

The benchmark dataset in [8] based on SSVEP-based Brain Computer Interface (BCI) is used for the validation of algorithms. It consists of 64-channel EEG data from 35 healthy subjects (8 experienced and 27 naive) and 40 stimulation frequencies ranging from 8 to 15.8 Hz with an interval of 0.2 Hz. For each subject, the experiment was performed in 6 blocks and each block consisted of 40 trials corresponding to 40 characters (26 English alphabets, 10 digits and 4 other symbols) indicated in random order. Each trial started with a visual cue indicating a target stimulus which appeared for 0.5 s on the screen and then all stimuli started to flicker on the screen concurrently and lasted for 5 s. The screen was kept blank for 0.5 s before the next trial began.

We used the same experimental setup as proposed in [11]. Measurement matrix $\Phi \in \mathbb{R}^{m \times n}$ was sparse binary matrix having each column with two entries of 1 in random locations while rest of the entries are 0. n was kept fixed and m was varied to meet desired Compression Ratio (CR) defined: $CR = \frac{n-m}{n} \times 100$.

For performance evaluation, we used *task-specific* performance evaluation where all the algorithms were evaluated based on their performances on frequency detection of SSVEPs using Canonical Correlation Analysis (CCA) [9]. In particular, at first, SSVEP detection was performed on the original dataset (which also serves as the baseline for algorithms) and then the same task was performed on the recovered dataset from few measurements using the algorithms.

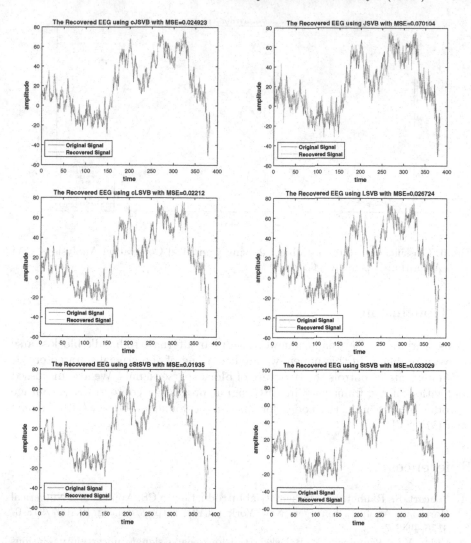

Fig. 5. Performance of Algorithms for EEG Reconstruction using 150 random measurements

For analysis, nine electrodes over the parietal and occipital areas (Pz, PO5, POz, PO4, PO6, O1, Oz and O2) were used. Number of harmonics for reference reconstruction was kept 3.

From Fig. 6, it is clear that cLSVB has outperformed in the experiment. Therefore, it can be seen that for CCA, around 40% (which corresponds to CR = 60) of the randomly sampled points were sufficient to correctly detect almost 90% (peak) of the letters for cLSVB based recovered EEG signals. For the sake of brevity, we present the result for Subject 2 but similar results were obtained for all the subjects. For more details of this work, please refer [12].

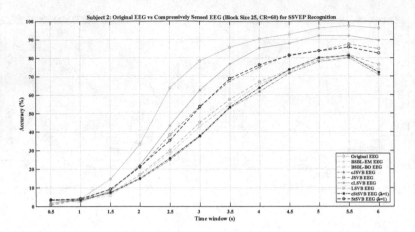

Fig. 6. Classification Rate for Subject 2 using Canonical Correlation Analysis (CCA) of all Algorithms when CR = 60

4   Conclusion

Sparse Variational Bayesian framework offers an alternate to handle block sparse recovery problem. In this paper, we analyzed one of the crucial parameters α_i which ultimately controls the structure of block sparse signals. We also discussed application of the framework in EEG signal processing context. To encourage reproducible research, the codes for [3] can be found at https://github.com/shruti51/cSVB.

References

1. Foucart, S., Rauhut, H.: Mathematical Introduction to CS: Applied and Numerical Harmonic Analysis. Springer, New York (2013). https://doi.org/10.1007/978-0-8176-4948-7
2. Eldar, Y.C., Kuppinger, P., Bolcskei, H.: Block-sparse signals: uncertainty relations and efficient recovery. IEEE Trans. Sig. Proc. **58**(6), 3042–3054 (2010)
3. Sharma, S., Chaudhury, S., Jayadeva: Variational Bayes block sparse modeling with correlated entries. In: 2018 24th International Conference on Pattern Recognition, pp. 1313–1318. ICPR, Beijing (2018)
4. Babacan, S.D., Nakajima, S., Do, M.N.: Bayesian group-sparse modeling and variational inference. IEEE Trans. Signal Proc. **62**(11), 2906–2921 (2014)
5. Zhang, Z., Rao, B.D.: Extension of SBL Algo. for the recovery of block sparse signals with intra-block correlation. IEEE Trans. Sig. Proc. **1**(8), 2009–2015 (2013)
6. Palamer, J.A., et al.: Variational EM algorithms for non-gaussian latent variable models. In: Proceedings of 18th International Conference on NIPS, pp. 1059–1066 (2005)
7. Zhang, Z., et al.: CS of EEG for wireless telemonitoring with low energy consumption and inexpensive hardware. IEEE Trans. Bio. Eng. **60**(1), 221–224 (2013)

8. Wang, Y., et al.: A benchmark dataset for SSVEP-based brain computer interfaces. IEEE Trans. Neural Syst. Rehab. Eng. **25**(10), 1746–1752 (2017)
9. Lin, Z., et al.: Frequency recognition based on CCA for SSVEP-based BCIs. IEEE Trans. Biomed. Eng. **54**(6), 1172–1176 (2007)
10. https://sites.google.com/site/researchbyzhang/publications
11. Zhang, Z., et al.: Spatio-temporal sparse Bayesian learning with applications to CS of multichannel physiological signals. IEEE Trans. Neural Syst. Rehab. Eng. **22**(6), 1186–1197 (2014)
12. Sharma S., Chaudhury S., Jayadeva: Temporal modeling of EEG signals using block sparse variational Bayes framework. In: 11th Indian Conference on Computer Vision, Graphics and Image Processing (ICVGIP), Hyderabad (2018)

Invited Reproducible Research Contributions

An Image Processing Library in Modern C++: Getting Simplicity and Efficiency with Generic Programming

Michaël Roynard[✉], Edwin Carlinet, and Thierry Géraud

EPITA Research and Development Laboratory, Le Kremlin-Bicêtre, France
{michael.roynard,edwin.carlinet,thierry.geraud}@lrde.epita.fr

Abstract. As there are as many clients as many usages of an Image Processing library, each one may expect different services from it. Some clients may look for efficient and production-quality algorithms, some may look for a large tool set, while others may look for extensibility and genericity to inter-operate with their own code base... but in most cases, they want a simple-to-use and stable product. For a C++ Image Processing library designer, it is difficult to conciliate genericity, efficiency and simplicity *at the same time*. Modern C++ (post 2011) brings new features for library developers that will help designing a software solution combining those three points. In this paper, we develop a method using these facilities to *abstract* the library components and augment the *genericity* of the algorithms. Furthermore, this method is not specific to image processing; it can be applied to any C++ scientific library.

Keywords: Image processing · Modern C++ · Generic programming · Efficiency · Simplicity · Concepts

1 Introduction

As many other numerical fields of computer science, *Computer Vision* and *Image Processing (IP)* have to face the constantly varying form of the input data. The data are becoming bigger and comes from a wider range of input devices: the current issue is generally not about acquiring data, but rather about handling and processing it (in a short time if possible...). In image processing, the two-dimensional RGB model has become too restrictive to handle the whole variety of *kinds* of image that comes with the variety of images fields. A non-exhaustive list of them includes: *remote sensing* (satellites may produce hyperspectral images with some thousands of bands), *medical imaging*, (scans may provide 3D and 3D+t volumes with several modalities), *virtual reality* (RGB-D cameras used for motion capture provide 2D/3D images with an extra 16-bits *depth* channel), *computational photography* (some high-dynamic-range sensors produce 32-bits images to preserve details in all ranges of the luminance)...

These examples already highlight the need for versatility, but some more domain-oriented applications attempt to broaden further the definition of

© Springer Nature Switzerland AG 2019
B. Kerautret et al. (Eds.): RRPR 2018, LNCS 11455, pp. 121–137, 2019.
https://doi.org/10.1007/978-3-030-23987-9_12

images. For example, in digital geometry, one would define images over non-regular domains as graphs, meshes or hexagonal grids. The increase of image type should not require to write several implementation of the algorithm. A single version should be able to work on several image types. The Fig. 1 illustrates this idea with the same watershed implementation applied on an image 2D, a graph as well as a mesh.

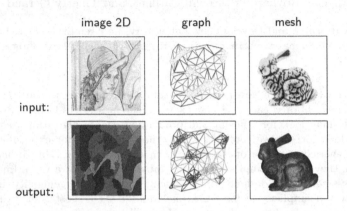

Fig. 1. Watershed algorithm applied to three images having different types.

Tools able to handle many data representations are said to be *generic*. In the particular case of a *library* providing a set of *routines*, *genericity* means that the *routines* can be applied to a variety of inputs (as opposed to *specific* routines that support inputs of unique *predefined* type). As an example, consider the morphological *dilation* that takes two inputs: an image and a flat structuring element (SE). Then, the set of some possible inputs is depicted in Fig. 2. Note that in this example, the image is already a type product between the underlying *structure kind* and the *value kind*. Let s be the number of structures, v the number of types of values, and k the number of structuring elements. With no *generalization*, one would have to write $s \times v \times k$ *dilation* routines.

Many IP libraries have emerged, developed in many programming languages. They all faced this problem and tried to bring solutions, some of which are reviewed in Sect. 2. Among these solutions, we see that *generic programming* is good starting point [15] to design a *generic* library but still has many problem. In particular, we focus on the case of MILENA [16,22], a generic pre-modern C++ IP libray and its shortcomings that led to the design of PYLENA [5]. The work presented in this paper contrasts with the previous works on obtaining genericity for mathematical morphology operators [8,21] and digital topology operators [23].

In Sect. 3, we present this new generic design, that emerged with the evolution of the Modern C++ and allowed solving some MILENA's shortcomings. Not only does this new design re-conciliate *simplicity* and *performance*, but it

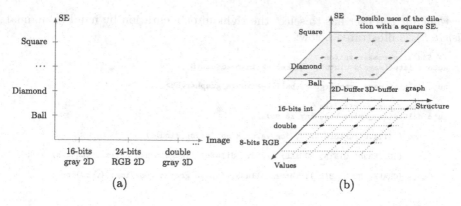

Fig. 2. The space of possible implementation of the *dilation(image, se)* routine. The image axis shown in (a) is in-fact multidimensional and should be considered 2D as in (b).

also promotes *extensibility* as it enables easily creating custom image types as those shown in Sect. 3.5.

2   Bringing Genericity in IP Libraries: Solutions and Problems

Generic programming aims at providing more flexibility to programs. It is itself a very *generic* term that means different things to different people. It may refer to *parametric polymorphism* (which is the common sense in C++), but it may also refer to *data abstraction* and *reflection /meta-programming* [17]. The accordance on a strict definition of *generic programming* is not our objective, but we can observe a manifestation of the *generic programming*: a parametrization of the routines to augment flexibility.

To tackle the problem of a *generic* dilation from the introduction, several programming techniques have been reviewed by Levillain et al. [24], Géraud [13]. We discuss these techniques w.r.t. some criteria: *usability* (simplicity from the end-user), *maintainability* (simplicity from the library developer stand-point), *run-time availability* (running routines on images whose *kind* is unknown until run-time), *efficiency* (speed and binary size tradeoff).

Ad-Hoc Polymorphism and Exhaustivity. The straightforward brute-force solution is the one that enumerates every combination of parameters. This means one implementation for each couple (*'image 'kind, 'structuring element 'kind*) and involves much code duplication. Both run-time or compile-time selection of the implementation are possible depending on the parametrization. If the *kind* of parameters are known at compile time (through their *type*), routine *overload* selection is automatically done by the compiler. On the contrary, if the *kind* of parameters are known at run-time (or if the language does not support *overloading*, the user has to select the right implementation by hand (a manual *dispatch*) as illustrated below:

```
// Static parametrization
auto dilate(image2d<uint8>, square) -> image2d<uint8>;
...
auto dilate(image_graph<rgb8>, ball) -> image_graph<rgb8>;

// Dynamic parametrization
auto dilate(any_image img, any_se se)
{
  switch ( (img.structure_kind, img.value_kind, se.se_kind) )
    {
    case (BUFFER2D, UINT8, SQUARE): return dilate( (image2d<uint8>)img, (square) se);
    ...
    case (GRAPH, RGB8, BALL): return dilate( (image_graph<rgb8>)img, (rgb8) se);
    }
}
```

Such a strategy is simple and efficient as the best implementation is written for each case. However it cannot scale, as any addition of a new kind (either a SE, a structure or a value type) would require duplicating many routines and lead to maintenance issues that is why no IP library has chosen such a strategy.

Generalization. A second approach is to generalize to the greatest common type (*a type to rule them all*) instead of augmenting their number. For example, one can consider that all *value types* are double since uint8, int16, ... can roughly be represented by double as in MEGAWAVE [10]. Even, if a library supports different *value kinds* for images, it is also common to use an *adapter* that performs a value conversion before calling a specific routine with the most general type. OpenCV [4] uses such an approach where one has to adapt his value types from one routine to another, which makes it painful to extend due to the wide variety of types and algorithms that this library has to offer. Dynamic data analysis framework as Matlab, Octave, Numpy/SciPy have many routines implemented for a single value type and convert their input if it does not fit the required type. The major drawback to this approach is a performance penalty due to conversions and processing on larger type.

Structures can also be generalized to a certain extent. In the image processing library CIMG, all images are 3-dimensional with an arbitrary number of channels. It leads to an interface where users can write ima(x,y,z,channel) even if the image has a single dimension. There are three drawbacks to this approach: the number of dimensions is bounded (cannot handle 3D+t for example), the interface allows the image to be used incorrectly (weak type-safety), every algorithm has to be written following a 4D pattern even if the image is only 2D. Moreover, *generalization* of *structures* is not trivial when they are really different (e.g. finding the common type between a 3D-buffer encoded image and an image over a graph).

Inclusion & Parametric Polymorphism. A common conception of *generic programming* relates the definitions of *abstractions* and *template methods*.

A first programming paradigm that enables such a distinction is *object oriented programming (OOP)*. In this paradigm, *template methods*, as defined by [11], are general routines agnostic to the implementation details and specific properties of a given type. A *template method* defines the skeleton of an algorithm with customization points (calls can be redefined to our own handlers) or we can plug our own types. Hence, *template methods* are *polymorphic*. They rely on the abality to *abstract* the behavior of objects we handle. The *abstraction* thus declares an *interface*: a set of services (generally *abstract methods*) which are common to all the *kinds*. The *concrete* types have then to define *abstract methods* with implementation details.

On the other hand, *generic programming*, in the sense of **(author?)** [25] provides another way of creating *abstraction* and *template methods*. In this paradigm, *the abstraction* is replaced by *a concept* that defines the set of operations a type must provide. *OOP template methods* are commonly refered as *template functions* and implement the algorithm in terms of the *concepts*.

While similar in terms of idea, the two paradigms should not be confused. On one hand, OOP relies on the *inclusion* polymorphism. A single routine (implementation) exists and supports any sub-type that inherits from the *abstract type* (which is the way of defining an *interface* in C++). Also, the *kind* of entities is not known until *run-time*, types are *dynamic* and so is the selection of the right method. This has to be compared to *generic programming* that relies on the *parametric* polymorphism, which is *static*. The *kinds* of entities have to be known at *compile time* and a version of the *template function* is created for each input types. In Fig. 3, we illustrate these differences through the implementation of the simple routine `copy` (`dilate` would require a more advanced abstraction of an image that will be detailed in Sect. 3). Basically, *copy* just has to traverse an input image and stores the values in an output image. The way of *abstracting* the traversal is done with *iterators*.

Run-time polymorphism offers a greater flexibility in *dynamic* environment, where the types of the image to handle are not known until the execution of the program. For example, *scipy.ndimage*, a python image processsing library for interactive environments, uses a C-stylished version of the iterator abstraction [28] and value abstraction given above (*C-style* stands for an hand-made *switch* dispatch instead of *virtual methods*). GEGL [1], used in GIMP, is also written in C ans uses C-style run-time polymorphism to achieve abstraction over colors and data buffers (e.g. to model graphs).

Nevertheless, this flexibility comes at the cost of degraded performances due to the *dynamic dispatches*. On the other hand, *static* polymorphism provides better performances because *concrete types* are known at compile time and there is no need to resolve *methods* at run-time. As there is never no free lunch, performance comes at the cost of less run-time flexibility. Moreover, since *parametric polymorphism* is implemented through *templates* in C++, many instanciations of the same code occur for different input types and may lead to *code bloat* and large executables.

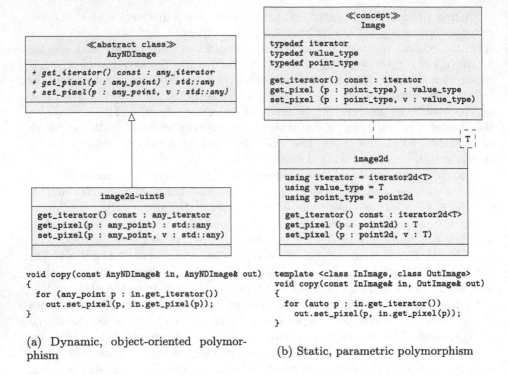

(a) Dynamic, object-oriented polymorphism

(b) Static, parametric polymorphism

Fig. 3. Comparison of the implementations of a polymorphic routine with the *object-oriented programming* and *generic programming* paradigms

Parametric Polymorphism in C++ Image Processing Libraries. Parametric polymorphism is common in many C++ IP libraries to a certain extent. Many of them, (e.g. CImg [34], Video++ [12], ITK [19]) provide *value type* genericity (e.g. `image2d<T>`) while a few provide a full structural genericity (DGTal [7], GrAL [2], Milena [24], VIGRA [20], Boost.GIL [3]). To reach such a level a genericity, these libraries have been written in a complex C++ which remains visible from the user standpoint. *Erich Gamma* [11] notice that *dynamic, highly parameterized software is harder to understand than more static software.* In particular, errors in highly templated code is hard to read and to debug because they show up very deep in the compiler error trace.

Also, they have not been written with the modern user-friendly features that the new C++ offers. Worst, in the case of Milena, some design choices made in pre-C++ 11, makes the library not compatible with the current standard and prevents usage of these new features.

Additionally, there exists other, non-library approach, such as designing a whole new DSL (Domain Specific Language) to reach a specific goal. For instance, Halide [29] chose this approach to fully focus on the underlying generated code to optimize it for vectorization, parallelism and data locality.

Unfortunately this implies trade-offs on genericity and interoperability as we are not dealing with native C++ anymore.

3   C++ Generic Programming and Concepts

C++ is a multi-paradigm language that enables the developer to write code that can be *object oriented, procedural, functional* and *generic*. However, there were limitations that were mostly due to the backward compatibility constraint as well as the zero-cost abstraction principle. In particular the *generic programming* paradigm is provided by the *template metaprogramming* machinery which can be rather obscure and error-prone. Furthermore, when the code is incorrect, due to the nature of templates (and the way they are specified) it is extremely difficult for a compiler to provide a clear and useful error message. To solve this issue, a new facility named *concepts* was brought to the language. It enables the developer to constraint types: we say that the type *models* the *concept(s)*. For instance, to compare two images, a function *compare* would restrict its input image types to the ones whose value type provides the *comparison operator* ==.

In spite of the history behind the *concept checking* facilities being very turbulent [30,32,33], it will finally appear in the next standard [35] (C++20).

3.1   From Algorithms to Concepts

The C++ *Standard Template Library* (STL) is a collection of algorithms and data structures that allow the developer to code with generic facilities. For instance, there is a standard way to *reduce* a collection of elements: `std::accumulate` that is agnostic to the underlying collection type. The collection just needs to provide a facility so that it can work. This facility is called *iterator*. All STL algorithms behave this way: the type is a template parameter so it can be anything. What is important is how this type behaves. Some collection requires you to define a `hash` functions (`std::map`), some requires you to set an *order* on your elements (`std::set`) etc. This emphasis the power of genericity. The most important point to remember here (and explained very early in 1988 [25]) is the answer to: "*What is a generic algorithm?*". The answer is: "*An algorithm is generic when it is expressed in the most abstract way possible*".

Later, in his book [31], Stepanov explained the design decision behind those algorithms as well as an important notion born in the early 2000s: the concepts. The most important point about concepts is that it constraints the behavior. Henceforth: "*It is not the types that define the concepts: it is the algorithms*".

The *Image Processing* and *Computer Vision* fields are facing this issue because there are a lot of algorithms, a lot of different kind of images and a lot of different kind of requirements/properties for those algorithms to work. In fact, when analyzing the algorithms, you can always extract those requirements in the form of one or several *concepts*.

3.2   Rewriting an Algorithm to Extract a Concept

Gamma Correction. Let us take the gamma correction algorithm as an example. The naive way to write this algorithm can be:

```
1    template <class Image>
2    void gamma_correction(Image& ima, double gamma)
3    {
4      const auto gamma_corr = 1 / gamma;
5
6      for (int x = 0; x < ima.width(); ++x)
7        for (int y = 0; y < ima.height(); ++y)
8        {
9          ima(x, y).r = std::pow((255 * ima(x, y).r) / 255, gamma_corr);
10         ima(x, y).g = std::pow((255 * ima(x, y).g) / 255, gamma_corr);
11         ima(x, y).b = std::pow((255 * ima(x, y).b) / 255, gamma_corr);
12       }
13   }
```

This algorithm here does the job but it also makse a lot of hypothesis. Firstly, we suppose that we can write in the image via the = operator (1.9–11): it may not be true if the image is sourced from a generator function. Secondly, we suppose that we have a 2D image via the double loop (1.6–7). Finally, we suppose we are operating on 8bits range (0–255) RGB via '.r', '.g', '.b' (1.9–11). Those hypothesis are unjustified. Intrinsically, all we want to say is *"For each value of ima, apply a gamma correction on it."*. Let us proceed to make this algorithm the most generic possible by lifting those unjustified constraints one by one.

Lifting RGB constraint: First, we get rid of the 8bits color range (0–255) RGB format requirement. The loops become:

```
using value_t = typename Image::value_type;

const auto gamma_corr = 1 / gamma;
const auto max_val = std::numeric_limits<value_t>::max();

for(int x = 0; x < ima.width(); ++x)
  for(int y = 0; y < ima.height(); ++y)
    ima(x, y) = std::pow((max_val * ima(x, y)) / max_val, gamma_corr);
```

By lifting this constraint, we now require the type Image to define a nested type `Image::value_type` (returned by `ima(x, y)`) on which `std::numeric_limits` and `std::pow` are defined. This way the compiler will be able to check the types at compile-time and emit warning and/or errors in case it detects incompatibilities. We are also able to detect it beforehand using a `static_assert` for instance.

Lifting bi-dimensional constraint: Here we need to introduce a new abstraction layer, the *pixel*. A *pixel* is a couple (*point, value*). The double loop then becomes:

```
for (auto&& pix : ima.pixels())
  pix.value() = std::pow((max_val * pix.value()) / max_val, gamma_corr);
```

This led to us requiring that the type *Image* requires to provide a method `Image::pixels()` that returns *something* we can iterate on with a range-for loop: this *something* is a *Range* of *Pixel*. This *Range* is required to behave like an *iterable*: it is an abstraction that provides a way to browse all the elements one by one. The *Pixel* is required to provide a method `Pixel::value()` that returns a *Value* which is *Regular* (see Sect. 3.3). Here, we use `auto&&` instead of `auto&` to allow the existence of proxy iterator (think of `vector<bool>`). Indeed, we may be iterating over a lazy-computed view Sect. 3.5.

Lifting writability constraint: Finally, the most subtle one is the requirement about the *writability* of the image. This requirement can be expressed directly via the new C++20 syntax for *concepts*. All we need to do is changing the template declaration by:

```
template <WritableImage Image>
```

In practice the C++ keyword `const` is not enough to express the *constness* or the *mutability* of an image. Indeed, we can have an image whose pixel values are returned by computing $cos(x + y)$ (for a 2D point). Such an image type can be instantiated as *non-const* in C++ but the values will not be *mutable*: this type will not model the *WritableImage* concept.

Final version

```
template <WritableImage Image>
void gamma_correction(Image& ima, double gamma)
{
  using value_t = typename Image::value_type;

  const auto gamma_corr = 1 / gamma;
  const auto max_val = numeric_limits<value_t>::max();

  for (auto&& pix : ima.pixels())
    pix.value() = std::pow((max_val * pix.value()) / max_val, gamma_corr);
}
```

When re-writing a lot of algorithms this way: lifting constraints by requiring behavior instead, we are able to deduce what our *concepts* needs to be. The real question for a *concept* is: *"what behavior should be required?"*

Dilation Algorithm. To show the versatility of this approach, we will now attempt to deduces the requirements necessary to write a classical *dilate* algorithm. First let us start with a naive implementation:

```
1    template <class InputImage, class OutputImage>
2    void dilate(const InputImage& input_ima, OutputImage& output_ima)
3    {
4      assert(input_ima.height() == output_ima.height()
5        && input_ima.width() == output_ima.width());
6
7      for (int x = 2; x < input_ima.width() - 2; ++x)
8        for (int y = 2; y < input_ima.height() - 2; ++y)
9        {
10         output_ima(x, y) = input_ima(x, y)
11         for (int i = x - 2; i <= x + 2; ++i)
12           for (int j = y - 2; j <= y + 2; ++j)
13             output_ima(x, y) = std::max(output_ima(x, y), input_ima(i, j));
14       }
15   }
```

Here we are falling into the same pitfall as for the *gamma correction* example: there are a lot of unjustified hypothesis. We suppose that we have a 2D image (1.7–8), that we can write in the `output_image` (1.10, 13). We also require that the input image does not handle borders, (cf. loop index arithmetic 1.7-8, 11-12). Additionally, the *structuring element* is restricted to a 5×5 window (1.11-12) whereas we may need to dilate via, for instance, a 11×15 window, or a sphere. Finally, the algorithm does not exploit any potential properties such as the *decomposability* (1.11-12) to improve its efficiency. Those hypothesis are, once again, unjustified. Intrinsically, all we want to say is "For each value of `input_ima`, take the maximum of the $X \times X$ window around and then write it in `output_ima`".

To lift those constraints, we need a way to know which kind of *structuring element* matches a specific algorithm. Thus, we will pass it as a parameter. Additionally, we are going to lift the first two constraints the same way we did for *gamma correction*:

```
template <Image InputImage, WritableImage OutputImage, StructuringElement SE>
void dilate(const InputImage& input_ima, OutputImage& output_ima, const SE& se)
{
  assert(input_ima.size() == output_ima.size());

  for(auto&& [ipix, opix] : zip(input_ima.pixels(), output_ima.pixels()))
  {
    opix.value() = ipix.value();
    for (const auto& nx : se(ipix))
      opix.value() = std::max(nx.value(), opix.value());
  }
}
```

We now do not require anything except that the *structuring element* returns the neighbors of a pixel. The returned value must be an *iterable*. In addition, this code uses the `zip` utility which allows us to iterate over two ranges at the same time. Finally, this way of writing the algorithm allows us to delegate the issue about the border handling to the neighborhood machinery. Henceforth, we will not address this specific point deeper in this paper.

3.3   Concept Definition

The more algorithms we analyze to extract their requirements, the clearer the *concepts* become. They are slowly appearing. Let us now attempt to formalize them. The formalization of the *concept Image* from the information and requirements we have now is shown in Table 1 for the required type definitions and valid expressions.

The *concept Image* does not provide a facility to write inside it. To do so, we have refined a second *concept* named *WritableImage* that provides the necessary facilities to write inside it. We say "*WritableImage* refines *Image*".

The *sub-concept ForwardRange* can be seen as a requirement on the underlying type. We need to be able to browse all the pixels in a forward way. Its *concept* will not be detailed here as it is very similar to *concept* of the same name [26, 27] (soon in the STL). Also, in practice, the *concepts* described here

Table 1. Formalization of concepts.

Let *Ima* be a type that models the concept *Image*. Let *WIma* be a type that models the concept *WritableImage*. Then *WIma* inherits all types defined for *Image*. Let *SE* be a type that models the concept *StructuringElement* . Let *DSE* be a type that models the concept *Decomposable*. Then *DSE* inherits all types defined for *StructuringElement*. Let *Pix* be a type that models the concept *Pixel*. Then we can define:

	Definition	Description	Requirement
Image	`Ima::const_pixel_range`	type of the range to iterate over all the constant pixels	models the concept *ForwardRange*
	`Ima::pixel_type`	type of a pixel	models the concept *Pixel*
	`Ima::value_type`	type of a value	models the concept *Regular*
Writable Image	`WIma::pixel_range`	type of the range to iterate over all the non-constant pixels	models the concept *ForwardRange*

Let *cima* be an instance of *const Ima*. Let *wima* be an instance of *WIma*. Then all the valid expressions defined for *Image* are valid for *WIma*. Let *cse* be an instance of *const SE*. Let *cdse* be an instance of *const DSE*. Then all the valid expressions defined for *StructuringElement* are valid for *const DSE* Let *cpix* be an instance of *const Pix*. Then we have the following valid expressions:

	Expression	Return Type	Description
Image	`cima.pixels()`	`Ima::const_pixel_range`	returns a range of constant pixels to iterate over it
Writable Image	`wima.pixels()`	`WIma::pixel_range`	returns a range of pixels to iterate over it
Structuring Element	`cse(cpix)`	`WIma::pixel_range`	returns a range of the neighboring pixels to iterate over it
Decomposable	`cdse.decompose()`	`implementation defined`	returns a range of structuring elements to iterate over it

are incomplete. We would need to analyze several other algorithms to deduce all the requirements so that our *concepts* are the most complete possible. One thing important to note here is that to define a simple *Image concept*, there are already a large amount of prerequisites: *Regular*, *Pixel* and *ForwardRange*. Those *concepts* are basic but are also tightly linked to the *concept* in the STL [6]. We refer to the STL *concepts* as *fundamental concepts*. *Fundamentals concepts* are the basic building blocks on which we work to build our own *concepts*. We show the C++20 code implementing those *concepts* in the code below.

```
template <class Ima>
concept Image = requires {
    typename Ima::value_type;
    typename Ima::pixel_type;
    typename Ima::const_pixel_range;
} && Regular<Ima::value_type>
&& ForwardRange<Ima::const_pixel_range>
&& requires(const Ima& cima) {
    { cima.pixels() }
        -> Ima::const_pixel_range;
};


template <class I>
using pixel_t = typename I::pixel_type;
template <class SE, class Ima>
concept StructuringElement = Image<Ima>
    && requires(const SE& cse,
            const pixel_t<Ima> cpix){
        { se(cpix) } -> Ima::const_pixel_range;
    };
```

```
template <class WIma>
concept WritableImage = requires Image<WIma>
&& requires {
    typename WIma::pixel_range;
} && ForwardRange<WIma::pixel_range>
&& ForwardRange<WIma::pixel_range,
        WIma::pixel_type>
&& requires(WIma& wima) {
    { wima.pixels() } -> WIma::pixel_range;
};


template <class DSE, class Ima>
concept Decomposable =
    StructuringElement<DSE, Ima>
    && requires(const DSE& cdse) {
        { cdse.decompose() }
            -> /*impl. defined*/;
    };
```

3.4   Specialization Vs. Properties

Another advantage of *concepts* are that they allow a *best match* machinery over requirement(s) met by a type. We call this mechanic the *property specialization*. It allows to select the correct overload (*best match* machinery) when the given template parameter satisfies the requirement(s) expressed via the concept(s). Historically we used the template specialization mechanism to achieve the same thing (via inheritance of specialized types and other tricks) but it came with lot of disadvantages. Those are the cost of the abstraction and indirection, the difficulty to extend as well as to inject new type or behavior for a new user, being tied to a type and finally, each new type needs its own new implementation. Switching to a property-based approach with an automatic *best match* machinery is much more efficient and user-friendly.

This machinery could be emulated pre-C++20 via cryptic template metapro- gramming tricks (i.e. type-traits, SFINAE and enable_if). However, C++20 brings a way to remove the need of these need, making it widely accessible. The code in Fig. 4 shows this difference in action.

```
template <class Image, class Value,
  std::enable_if_t<
    is_writable_image_v<Image>
    && is_value_v<Value>
    && !is_image_v<Image>>* = nullptr>
Image operator+(Image ima, Value v)
{
  for (auto&& pix : ima.pixels())
    pix.value() += v;
  return ima;
}

template <class ImLhs, class ImRhs,
  std::enable_if_t<
    is_writable_image_v<ImLhs>
    && !is_value_v<ImRhs>
    && is_image_v<ImRhs>>* = nullptr>
ImLhs operator+(ImLhs lhs, const ImRhs& rhs)
{
  for (auto&& [p_lhs, p_rhs] : zip(lhs, rhs))
    p_lhs.value() += p_rhs.value();
  return lhs;
}
```

```
template <WritableImage Ima, Value V>
Ima operator+(Ima ima, V v)
{
  for (auto&& pix : ima.pixels())
    pix.value() += v;
  return ima;
}

template <WritableImage ImLhs, Image Rhs>
ImLhs operator+(ImLhs lhs, const Rhs& rhs)
{
  for (auto&& [p_lhs, p_rhs] : zip(lhs, rhs))
    p_lhs.value() += p_rhs.value();
  return lhs;
}
```

Fig. 4. C++17 SFINAE trick vs. C++20 Concepts.

The result about which code is clearer, easier to read and less error-prone should be obvious. The first advantage is that the compiler do the *type-checking* pass early when instantiating the template instead of waiting until the *overload resolution* pass (the improper functions candidate are removed from *overload resolution* thanks to *SFINAE*). This directly *enhances the error messages* emitted by the compiler. Instead of having a long error trace one needs to scroll down to find the error within, the compiler will now emits the error first at the top with the incorrect *behavior requirement* that does not match the *concept* for a given instantiated type.

Also, in the C++17 code, with heavy *metaprograming trick*, informations about function prototypes such as *return type, parametric types* and *input types* are fuzzy and not very clear. It needs carefully designed and written user documentation to be usable by a tier. Furthermore, this documentation is often difficult to generate and documentation generators do not help because they have a very limited understanding of templated code. However, we can see in the C++20 code that, with *concepts*, we just have two different *overloads* with a single piece of information changing: the 2nd input parameter. The information is clear and can be easily understood by documentation generators.

In addition, as *concepts* are working with a *best-match* machinery, we can notice that it is not the case with the SFINAE tricks version. Each time you add a new variant, every possibilities, incompatibilities and ambiguities between all the overloads have to be manually lifted. Not doing so will lead to multiple overloads ambiguities (or none selected at all). Also, the compiler will issue a non-friendly error message difficult to address.

In *Image Processing* we are able to make use of this machinery, in particular with a property on *structuring elements*: the *decomposability*. For reminder a multi-dimensional *structuring element* is *decomposable* if it can be rewritten as many simpler *structuring elements*.

Indeed when the *structuring element* window is tiny, it makes little sense to exploit this property for efficiency. If instead of browsing the image once while selecting 4 neighbors for each pixel, then we browse the image twice while selecting 2 neighbors for each pixel, the difference is not relevant. However, the more the *structuring element* window grows, the more neighboring pixels are selected for each pixel. With a multi-dimensional *structuring element* the growth is quadratic whereas it is linear if the *structuring element* is *decomposed*.

Henceforth, bringing the *property best-match* machinery with *concepts* as well as this *decomposable* property lead us to this dilate algorithm version:

```
template <Image I, WritableImage O, StructuringElement SE> requires Decomposable<SE>
void dilate(const I& input, O& output, const SE& large_se)
{
  auto tmp = copy(input);
  for (auto&& small_se : large_se.decompose())
  {
    for (auto&& [ipix, opix] : zip(tmp.pixels(), output.pixels()))
    {
      opix.val() = ipix.val();
      for (auto&& nbx : small_se(ipix))
        opix.val() = std::max(opix.val(), nbx.val());
    }
    std::swap(tmp, output);
  }
  std::swap(tmp, output);
}
```

It is much more efficient as it reduces the complexity dramatically when the structuring element has a large selection window.

3.5   Practical Genericity for Efficiency: The Views

Let us introduce another key point enabled by genericity and concepts: the *Views*. A *View* is defined by a non-owning lightweight image, inspired by the design introduced in *Ranges for the Standard Library* [9] proposal for *non-owning collections*. A similar design is also called *Morphers* in MILENA [13, 21]. *Views* feature the following properties: *cheap to copy*, *non-owner* (does not *own* any data buffer), *lazy evaluation* (accessing the value of a pixel may require computations) and *composition*. When chained, the compiler builds a *tree of expressions* (or *expression template* as used in many scientific computing libraries such as Eigen [18]), thus it knows at compile-time the type of the composition and ensures a 0-overhead at evaluation.

There are four fundamental kind of views, inspired by functional programming paradigm: `transform(input, f)` applies the transformation *f* on each pixel of the image *input*, `filter(input, pred)` keeps the pixels of *input* that satisfy the predicate *pred*, `subimage(input, domain)` keeps the pixels of *input* that are in the domain *domain*, $zip(input_1, input_2, \ldots, input_n)$ allows to pack several pixel of several image to iterate on them all at the same time.

Lazy-evaluation combined with the view *chaining* allows the user to write clear and very efficient code whose evaluation is delayed till very last moment as shown in the code below (see [14] for additional examples). Neither memory allocation nor computation are performed; the image *i* has just recorded all the operations required to compute its values.

```
image2d<rgb8>  ima1 = /* ... */;
image2d<uint8_t> ima2 = /* ... */;

// Projection: project the red channel value
auto f = view::transform(ima, [](auto v) {
  return v.r;
});

// Lazy-evaluation of the element-wise
// minimum
auto g = view::transform(view::zip(f, ima2),
  [](auto value) {
    return std::min(std::get<0>(value),
          std::get<1>(value));
});
```

```
// Lazy-Filtering: keep pixels whose value
// is below < 128
auto h = view::filter(g, [] (auto value) {
  return value < 128;
}));

// Lazy-evaluation of a gamma correction
using value_t = typename Image::value_type;
constexpr float gamma = 2.2f;
constexpr auto max_val =
  std::numeric_limits<value_t>::max();
auto i = view::transform(h,
  [gamma_corr = 1 / gamma] (auto value) {
    return std::pow(value / max_val,
          gamma_corr) * max_val;
});
```

4   Conclusion and Perspectives

Through a simple example, we have shown a step-by-step methodology to make an algorithm *generic* with zero overhead[1]. To reach such a level of genericity and be able to write versatile algorithms, we had to *abstract* and *define* the most simple and fundamental elements of the libray (e.g. *image*, *pixel*, *structuring element*). We have shown that some tools of the Modern C++, such as *concepts*, greatly facilitate the definition and the usage of such abstractions. These tools

---

[1] The zero-cost abstraction of our approach is not argued here but will be discussed in an incoming paper with a comparison with the state of the art libraries.

enable the library designer to focus on the abstraction of the library components and on the user-visible development. The complex *template meta-programming* layer that used to be a large part of *C++ generic programming* is no more inevitable. In this context, it is worth pointing out the approach is not limited Image Processing libraries but works for any library that wants to be modernized to augment its productivity.

As one may have noticed, the solution presented in this paper is mostly dedicated to C++ developer and C++ end-user. Unlike dynamic environments (such as Python), C++ is not the most appropriate language when one has to prototype or experiment an IP solution. As a future work, we will study the conciliation of the *static genericity* from C++ (where types have to be known at compile time) with a *dynamic* language (with a run-time polymorphism) to allows the interactive usage of a C++ generic library.

References

1. Generic Graphic Library
2. Berti, G.: GrAL-the grid algorithms library. Future Gener. Comput. Syst. **22**(1–2), 110–122 (2006)
3. Bourdev, L., Jin, H.: Boost generic image library. In: Adobe Stlab (2006). Available at https://stlab.adobe.com/gil/index.html
4. Bradski, G.: The OpenCV Library. Dr. Dobb's J. Softw. Tools **120**, 122–125 (2000)
5. Carlinet, E., et al.: Pylena: a modern C++ image processing generic library. EPITA Research and Developement Laboratory (2018). Available at https://gitlab.lrde. epita.fr/olena/pylene
6. Carter, C., Niebler, E.: Standard library concepts June 2018. https://wg21.link/ p0898r3
7. Coeurjolly, D., Lachaud, J.O.: DGtal: Digital geometry tools and algorithms library. http://dgtal.org
8. Darbon, J., Géraud, T., Duret-Lutz, A.: Generic implementation of morphological image operators. In: Proceedings of the 6th International Symposium of Mathematical Morphology (ISMM), pp. 175–184. Sydney, Australia (2002)
9. Eric N., Sean Parent, A.S.: Ranges for the standard library: Revision 1, October 2014. https://ericniebler.github.io/std/wg21/D4128.html
10. Froment, J.: MegaWave. In: IPOL 2012 Meeting on Image Processing Libraries (2012)
11. Gamma, E.: Design Patterns: Elements of Reusable Object-Oriented Software. Pearson Education India, Chennai (1995)
12. Garrigues, M., Manzanera, A.: Video++, a modern image and video processing C++ framework. In: Conference on Design and Architectures for Signal and Image Processing (DASIP), pp. 1–6. IEEE (2014)
13. Géraud, T.: Outil logiciel pour le traitement d'images: Bibliothèque, paradigmes, types et algorithmes. Habilitation thesis, Université Paris-Est (2012). (in French)
14. Géraud, T., Carlinet, E.: A modern C++ library for generic and efficient image processing. Journée du Groupe de Travail de Géométrie Discrète et Morphologie Mathématique, Lyon, France, June 2018. https://www.lrde.epita.fr/theo/talks/ geraud.2018.gtgdmm_talk.pdf

15. Géraud, T., Fabre, Y., Duret-Lutz, A., Papadopoulos-Orfanos, D., Mangin, J.F.: Obtaining genericity for image processing and pattern recognition algorithms. In: Proceedings of the 15th International Conference on Pattern Recognition (ICPR). vol. 4, pp. 816–819. Barcelona, Spain (2000)
16. Géraud, T., Levillain, R., Lazzara, G.: The Milena image processing library. IPOL meeting, ENS Cachan, France, June 2012. https://www.lrde.epita.fr/~theo/talks/geraud.2012.ipol_talk.pdf
17. Gibbons, J.: Datatype-generic programming. In: Backhouse, R., Gibbons, J., Hinze, R., Jeuring, J. (eds.) SSDGP 2006. LNCS, vol. 4719, pp. 1–71. Springer, Heidelberg (2007). https://doi.org/10.1007/978-3-540-76786-2_1
18. Guennebaud, G., Jacob, B., et al.: Eigen v3. http://eigen.tuxfamily.org (2010). Available at http://eigen.tuxfamily.org
19. Ibanez, L., Schroeder, W., Ng, L., Cates, J.: The ITK software guide (2005)
20. Köthe, U.: Generic Programming for Computer Vision: The VIGRA Computer Vision Library. University of Hamburg, Cognitive Systems Group, Hamburg (2003)
21. Levillain, R., Géraud, T., Najman, L.: Milena: write generic morphological algorithms once, run on many kinds of images. In: Wilkinson, M.H.F., Roerdink, J.B.T.M. (eds.) ISMM 2009. LNCS, vol. 5720, pp. 295–306. Springer, Heidelberg (2009). https://doi.org/10.1007/978-3-642-03613-2_27
22. Levillain, R., Géraud, T., Najman, L.: Why and how to design a generic and efficient image processing framework: the case of the milena library. In: Proceedings of the IEEE International Conference on Image Processing (ICIP), pp. 1941–1944. Hong Kong September 2010 (2010)
23. Levillain, R., Géraud, T., Najman, L.: Writing reusable digital topology algorithms in a generic image processing framework. In: Köthe, U., Montanvert, A., Soille, P. (eds.) WADGMM 2010. LNCS, vol. 7346, pp. 140–153. Springer, Heidelberg (2012). https://doi.org/10.1007/978-3-642-32313-3_10
24. Levillain, R., Géraud, T., Najman, L., Carlinet, E.: Practical genericity: writing image processing algorithms both reusable and efficient. In: Proceedings of the 19th Iberoamerican Congress on Pattern Recognition (CIARP). LNCS, vol. 8827, pp. 70–79. Puerto Vallarta, Mexico (2014)
25. Backhouse, R., Gibbons, J. (eds.): Generic Programming. LNCS, vol. 2793. Springer, Heidelberg (2003). https://doi.org/10.1007/b12027
26. Niebler, E., Carter, C.: Deep integration of the ranges TS, May 2018. https://wg21.link/p1037r0
27. Niebler, E., Carter, C.: Merging the ranges TS, May 2018. https://wg21.link/p0896r1
28. Oliphant, T.E.: Multidimensional iterators in NumPy. In: Oram, A., Wilson, G. (eds.) Beautiful Code, vol. 19. O'reilly, Sebastopol (2007)
29. Ragan-kelley, J., Barnes, C., Adams, A., Durand, F., Amarasinghe, S., et al.: Halide: a language and compiler for optimizing parallelism, locality, and recomputation in image processing pipelines. In: PLDI **2013**, (2013)
30. Seymour, B.: LWG papers to re-merge into C++0x after removing concepts July 2009. https://wg21.link/n2929
31. Stepanov, A., McJones, P.: Elements of Programming. Addison-Wesley Professional, Boston (2009)
32. Stroustrup, B., Reis, G.D.: Concepts - Design choices for template argument checking, October 2003. https://wg21.link/n1522

33. Sutton, A.: Working draft, C++ extensions for concepts, June 2017. https://wg21.link/n4674
34. Tschumperlé, D.: The CImg library. IPOL 2012 Meeting on Image Processing Libraries (2012)
35. Voutilainen, V.: Merge the concepts TS working draft into the C++20 working draft, June 2017. https://wg21.link/p0724r0

New Definition of Quality-Scale Robustness for Image Processing Algorithms, with Generalized Uncertainty Modeling, Applied to Denoising and Segmentation

Antoine Vacavant[1]([✉]), Marie-Ange Lebre[1], Hugo Rositi[1],
Manuel Grand-Brochier[1], and Robin Strand[2]

[1] Université Clermont Auvergne, CNRS, SIGMA Clermont, Institut Pascal, 63000
Clermont-Ferrand, France
antoine.vacavant@uca.fr
[2] CBA, Uppsala Universitet, Uppsala, Sweden
robin.strand@it.uu.se

Abstract. Robustness is an important concern in machine learning and pattern recognition, and has attracted a lot of attention from technical and scientific viewpoints. Actually, the robustness models the capacity of a computerized approach to resist to perturbing phenomena and data uncertainties, and generate common artefact while designing algorithms. However, this question has not been dealt in depth in such a way for image processing tasks. In this article, we propose a novel definition of robustness dedicated to image processing algorithms. By considering a generalized model of image data uncertainty, we encompass the classic additive Gaussian noise alteration that we study through the evaluation of image denoising algorithms, but also more complex phenomena such as shape variability, which is considered for liver volume segmentation from medical images. Furthermore, we refine our evaluation of robustness wrt. our previous work by introducing a novel quality-scale definition. To do so, we calculate the worst loss of quality for a given algorithm over a set of uncertainty scales, together with the scale where this drop appears. This new approach permits to reveal any algorithm's weakness, and for which kind of corrupted data it may happen.

Keywords: Image processing · Robustness · Image denoising · Liver segmentation

1 Introduction

Reproducibility and robustness are important concerns in image processing and pattern recognition tasks, and for various applications such as medical image analysis for instance [18,26]. While the first refers to the replicable reuse of a

B. Kerautret et al. (Eds.): RRPR 2018, LNCS 11455, pp. 138–149, 2019.
https://doi.org/10.1007/978-3-030-23987-9_13

method (and generally a code) by associating input image data and method's outputs [17], the second is generally understood as the ability of an algorithm to resist to uncontrolled phenomena and to data uncertainties, such as image noise [29]. This article focuses on the evaluation of this robustness, which is a crucial matter in machine learning and computer vision [2,21] and increasingly with the emergence of deep learning algorithms [3,6] and big data [22,25]. However, in the field of image processing, this definition of robustness and its evaluation have not been further studied in such a way. The first definition we have proposed in RRPR 2016 [28] (called α-robustness) was the first attempt in measuring robustness by considering multiple scales of noise, and applied to two tasks: still image denoising and background subtraction in videos. In this previous work, image data was supposed to be altered by an additive Gaussian (or equivalent) noise, which is a common hypothesis when we refer to noisy image content. This robustness measurement consisted in calculating the worst quality loss (the α value) of a given algorithm, for a set of noise scales (e.g. increasing standard deviation of a Gaussian noise).

In the present article, we introduce in Sect. 2 a novel quality-scale definition of robustness still dedicated to image processing algorithms, by a generalized model of the pertubating phenomenon under consideration. Instead of representing only additive Gaussian noises, we can consider more complex *image data uncertainties*. To be able to evaluate robustness, we only need to measure data uncertainty by a monotonic increasing function. Moreover, together with the α value presented earlier, we also calculate the scale of uncertainty (σ) that generated an algorithm's worst loss of quality. Then, we apply this definition (called (α, σ)-robustness) first by revisiting the topic of image enhancement and denoising with the parallel concern of representation of noise in a multi-scale manner (Sect. 3), as we did in [28]. In this context the uncertainty is modeled as a classic Gaussian noise. Second we study the impact of shape variability in liver volume segmentation from medical images (Sect. 4). Here, we also propose to measure the uncertainty (liver variability) by a monotonic function, thus adapted to our test of robustness. In Sect. 5, we describe the code that can be publicly downloaded in [24] to reproduce the results of this paper, and so that any reader may evaluate the robustness of image processing methods. We conclude and enlarge the viewpoint of this paper by proposing future axes of progress of this research in Sect. 6.

2 A Novel Definition of Robustness for Image Processing

We first consider that an algorithm designed for image processing may be perturbed, because of an input data altered with a given uncertainty. By extending notations from the work [20,28], we pose:

$$\widehat{y_i} = y_i^0 \odot \delta y_i, \ y_i \in \mathbb{R}^q, \ i = 1,\ldots,n, \tag{1}$$

which will be shortened by $\widehat{\mathbf{Y}} = \mathbf{Y^0} \odot \delta \mathbf{Y}$ when the context allows it, i.e. when the subscripts are not necessary. The measurement $\widehat{\mathbf{Y}}$ is obtained from a perfect value $\mathbf{Y^0}$, corrupted by the alteration $\delta\mathbf{Y}$. Classically, $\delta\mathbf{Y}$ may be considered as a Gaussian noise by supposing that $\delta y_i \simeq GI(0, \sigma^2 C_y)$ where $\sigma^2 C_y$ is the covariance of the errors at a known noise scale σ (*e.g.* standard deviation or std.). This noise is generally added to the input data so that $\widehat{\mathbf{Y}} = \mathbf{Y^0} + \delta\mathbf{Y}$. Section 3 explores this classic scenario of additive noise modeling.

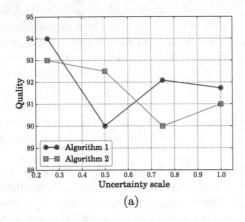

Name	(α, σ)
Algorithm 1	(16.0,0.25)
Algorithm 2	(10.0,0.5)

(b)

(a)

Fig. 1. Evaluation of the (α, σ)-robustness with a synthetic example with two algorithms compared by graphical inspection (a) where we can observe the most severe decrease of quality for Algorithm 1, and confirmed by the numerical evaluation (b).

In this article, we also consider more complex phenomena that do not refer to this model. In such difficult situations, alteration $\delta\mathbf{Y}$ and operator $\odot$ cannot be modeled theoretically or numerically evaluated, and we only know the measures $\widehat{\mathbf{Y}}$ and the perfect case $\mathbf{Y^0}$. A way to model the uncertainty is to define a variability scale σ between a given sample $\widehat{\mathbf{Y}}$ and the perfect, standard case $\mathbf{Y^0}$. In Sect. 4, we propose to study shape variability through this viewpoint.

Let A be an algorithm dedicated to image processing, leading to an output $\mathbf{X} = \{x_i\}_{i=1,n}$ (in general the image resulting from the algorithm). Let N be an uncertainty specific to the target application of this algorithm, and $\{\sigma_k\}_{k=1,m}$ the scales of N. The different outputs of A for every scale of N is $\mathbb{X} = \{\mathbf{X_k}\}_{k=1,m}$. The ground truth is denoted by $\mathbb{Y}^0 = \{\mathbf{Y_k^0}\}_{k=1,m}$. Let $Q(\mathbf{X_k}, \mathbf{Y_k^0})$ be a quality measure of A for scale k of N. This Q function's parameters are the result of A and the ground truth for a noise scale k. An example can be the F-measure, combining true and false positive and negative detections for a binary decision (as binary segmentation for instance). Our new definition of robustness can be formalized as follows:

Definition 1 ((α, σ)-robustness). Algorithm A is considered as robust if the difference between the output $\mathbb{X}$ and ground truth $\mathbb{Y}^0$ is bounded by a Lipschitz continuity of the Q function:

$$d_Y\left(Q(\mathbf{X_k}, \mathbf{Y_k^0}), Q(\mathbf{X_{k+1}}, \mathbf{Y_{k+1}^0})\right) \leq \alpha d_X(\sigma_{k+1}, \sigma_k), \ 1 \leq k < m, \qquad (2)$$

where

$$d_Y\left(Q(\mathbf{X_k}, \mathbf{Y_k^0}), Q(\mathbf{X_{k+1}}, \mathbf{Y_{k+1}^0})\right) = Q(\mathbf{X_{k+1}}, \mathbf{Y_{k+1}^0}) - Q(\mathbf{X_k}, \mathbf{Y_k^0}),$$
$$d_X(\sigma_{k+1}, \sigma_k) = |\sigma_{k+1} - \sigma_k|. \tag{3}$$

We calculate the robustness measure (α, σ) of A as the α value obtained and the scale $\sigma = \sigma_k$ where this value is reached.

In other words, α measures the worst drop in quality through the scales of uncertainty $\{\sigma_k\}$, and σ keeps the uncertainty scale leading to this value. The most robust algorithm should have a low α value, and a very high σ value. Figure 1 is a synthetic example of evaluation of two algorithms with this definition. This example illustrates the better robustness of Algorithm 2, since its α value is smaller than the one of Algorithm 1. Moreover, we can precise that this robustness is achieved for a larger value of uncertainty with the σ value.

3 Application to Image Enhancement and Denoising

Image denoising has been addressed by a wide range of methodologies, which can be appreciated in a general manner in [16] for instance. The shock filter [23] is a PDE scheme that consists in employing morphological operators depending on the sign of the Laplacian operator. The original algorithm is not able to reduce image noise accurately, but several authors have improved it for this purpose. As summarized in Fig. 2-b, our test of robustness concerns these approaches based on shock scheme [1,7,30]; another PDE-based algorithm named coherence filtering [32]; together with the classic median [12] and bilateral [27] filterings; and an improved version of the median filter [14]. We use 13 very famous images (*Barbara, Airplane, etc.*), with additive white Gaussian noise altering them with varying kernel std., by considering the scales of noise $\{\sigma_k\} = \{5, 10, 15, 20, 25\}$. The quality measure is the SSIM (structural similarity) originally introduced by [31].

Thanks to Definition 1, we are able to evaluate the robustness of various algorithms (Fig. 2), from a visual assessment thanks to the graph in Fig. 2(a), or numerically by getting the (α, σ) values as in (b).

Since we consider an additive noise ($\widehat{\mathbf{Y}} = \mathbf{Y^0} + \delta\mathbf{Y}$ with our notations), quality functions are decreasing monotonically over the set of noise scales, revealing that the tested algorithms loose progressively their efficiency. We can appreciate the good behavior of the algorithms SmoothedMedian and SmoothedShock, with a lower α value and a larger σ scale than the other approaches, which means that the worst quality decrease has been observed when an aggressive Gaussian noise is applied to images.

Figure 3 presents the outputs obtained for all algorithms of our test. This confirms the good image enhancement achieved by the most robust methods, SmoothedMedian and SmoothedShock.

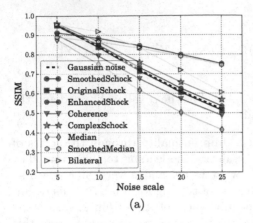

Name	Ref.	(α, σ)
Median	[12]	(0.027,10)
OriginalShock	[23]	(0.025,10)
Coherence	[32]	(0.024,10)
EnhancedShock	[1]	(0.023,10)
Bilateral	[27]	(0.023,15)
ComplexShock	[7]	(0.022,10)
SmoothedMedian	[14]	(0.009,20)
SmoothedShock	[30]	(0.009,20)

(b)

(a)

Fig. 2. Evaluation of (α, σ)-robustness for image denoising algorithms, by studying quality function decrease through scales of noise (a) or numerically by appreciating the (α, σ) values for each algorithm.

4   Application to Liver Volume Segmentation

Liver segmentation has been addressed by various approaches in the literature [11], and mostly oriented towards CT (computerized tomography) modality (see *e.g.* [10]). We propose to compare two liver extraction approaches in this test of robustness. The automatic model-based algorithm presented in [15] (named hereafter MultiVarSeg) is based on the prior 3-D representation of any patient's liver by accumulating images from diverse public datasets. We compare MultiVarSeg with a free available semi-automatic segmentation software, called SmartPaint [19]. It allows a fully interactive segmentation of medical volume images based on region growing.

To compare these methods, we employ the datasets provided by the Research Institute against Digestive Cancer (IRCAD) [13] and by the SLIVER benchmark [11]. We propose to study the uncertainty of liver shape variability, revealing this organ's complex and variable geometry. First, we construct a bounding box (BB) with standard dimensions of the liver certified by an expert and computed by the mean values of our database. We measure the liver variability of a given binary image (object of interest -the liver- vs. background) by the following function:

$$\sigma = \frac{\#(L \setminus BB)}{\#(L)} \times 100, \qquad (4)$$

where L is the set of pixels that belong to the liver in a binary segmentation. $L \setminus BB$ represents pixels that belong to the liver measured outside the standard box BB. The operator $\#(.)$ stands for the cardinality of sets. To compare the tested algorithms, we use the Dice coefficient, which is a very common way to measure the accuracy of any segmentation method.

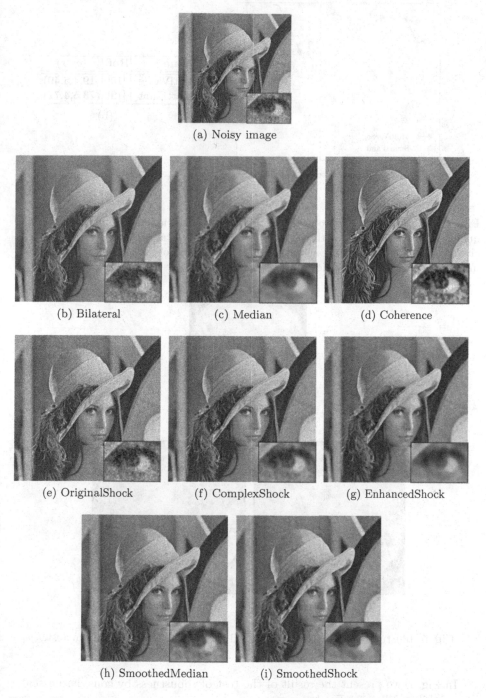

(a) Noisy image

(b) Bilateral   (c) Median   (d) Coherence

(e) OriginalShock   (f) ComplexShock   (g) EnhancedShock

(h) SmoothedMedian   (i) SmoothedShock

Fig. 3. Illustrations of the results obtained for all the image denoising algorithms of our test.

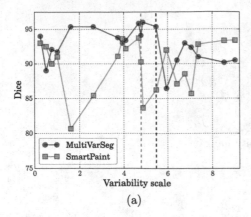

Name	Ref.	(α, σ)
MultiVarSeg	[15]	(19.4,5.49)
SmartPaint	[19]	(73.5,4.71)

(b)

(a)

Fig. 4. Evaluation of (α, σ)-robustness for liver segmentation algorithms, by studying quality function fluctuations through scales of variability (a) or numerically by appreciating the (α, σ) values for each algorithm. The scale σ obtained for each algorithm in (b) is depicted with a vertical dotted line in (a).

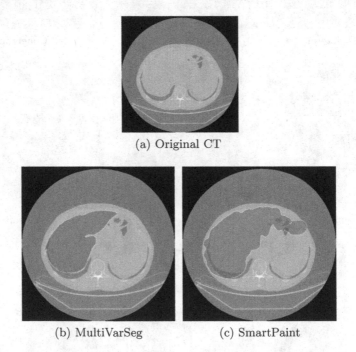

(a) Original CT

(b) MultiVarSeg   (c) SmartPaint

Fig. 5. Illustration of the results obtained by the two algorithms of our test.

In Fig. 4, we present the result of the test of robustness by considering scale of variability following Eq. 4.

We consider here a more complex phenomenon producing uncertainty upon image data (general formalism $\widehat{\mathbf{Y}} = \mathbf{Y^0} \odot \delta\mathbf{Y}$), measured by a variability function. It provokes non-linear quality functions for both algorithms, however our definition of robustness enables the assessment in this case. We can thus observe the robustness of MultiVarSeg compared to SmartPaint, by a lower α and a larger σ values.

In Fig. 5 are depicted the segmentation results obtained for each tested method. This visual inspection permits to confirm the accuracy of the model-based approach MultiVarSeg.

5   Reproducibility

We have developed a Python code, provided publicly in [24], which permits to assess visually and numerically robustness of image processing techniques. The reader can thus reproduce the plots and tables of Figs. 1, 2 and 4 of this paper. These elements are automatically created by means of the input data files presented as in Fig. 6.

Such files are composed of: the quality measure in the first line; in the second line the name of noise or uncertainty to be studied, followed by values of scales; then the next lines concern quality values of the tested algorithms, with their name at the first position, line by line until the end of the file.

Once any user runs:

```
python measure_robustness.py rip_test_image_filtering.dat
```

for instance, our program will provide a plot displayed and saved as 'fig_rob.pdf'; a LaTeX file named 'tab_rob.tex' containing the table with values of (α, σ)-robustness in decreasing order of α; it will also print these values in the console (see Fig. 6-d).

To obtain these measures, our program first calculates α according to Definition 1. To do so, we can rewrite Eq. 2 to determine α as:

$$\alpha \geq \frac{d_Y\left(Q(\mathbf{X_k}, \mathbf{Y_k^0}), Q(\mathbf{X_{k+1}}, \mathbf{Y_{k+1}^0})\right)}{d_X(\sigma_{k+1}, \sigma_k)}, \ 1 \leq k < m. \tag{5}$$

The denominator $d_X(\sigma_{k+1}, \sigma_k)$ does not equal zero, this is easily ensured by always considering distinct scales of uncertainty, i.e. by assuming wlog. That $\sigma_{k+1} > \sigma_k$, $1 \leq k < m$. We could select any value of α satisfying this equation, however, we prefer a reproducible strategy by computing the maximal value:

$$\alpha = \max_{1 \leq k < m}\left\{\frac{d_Y\left(Q(\mathbf{X_k}, \mathbf{Y_k^0}), Q(\mathbf{X_{k+1}}, \mathbf{Y_{k+1}^0})\right)}{d_X(\sigma_{k+1}, \sigma_k)}\right\}. \tag{6}$$

During this process, we also store the uncertainty scale σ where this α value has been reached.

```
Quality
Uncertainty scale    0.25   0.5  0.75   1
Algorithm 1  94   90   92.1  91.7
Algorithm 2  93   92.5   90   91
```

(a) `rip_test_first_sample.dat`

```
SSIM
Gaussian noise scale   5   10   15   20   25
SmoothedShock  0.9131   0.8841   0.8457   0.7990   0.7523
SmoothedMedian  0.8900   0.8668   0.8325   0.7907   0.7454
EnhancedShock  0.9532   0.8504   0.7330   0.6256   0.5343
ComplexShock   0.9599   0.8678   0.7599   0.6576   0.5681
OriginalShock  0.9496   0.8381   0.7154   0.6053   0.5132
Coherence  0.9021   0.7931   0.6750   0.5716   0.4870
Median  0.8776   0.7507   0.6162   0.5028   0.4144
Bilateral  0.9559   0.9198   0.8352   0.7199   0.6058
```

(b) `rip_test_image_filtering.dat`

```
Dice
Liver variability 0.25   0.5  0.75   1  1.6  2.63   3.74   3.95   4.1  4.69
4.79   4.88   5.49   5.95   6.42   6.77   7.06   7.37   8.52   9
MultiVar  94   90   92.0916  91.732   95.3708  95.3721  93.7945  92.985   93.4042  95.8556
94.1146  96.0183  95.3639  86.4506  90.5175  92.9795  92.3665  90.9774  90.1586  90.4932
SmartPaint   93   92.5   90   91   80.6671  85.4201  91.0875  93.6161  92.2028  93.7228
90.2645  83.6534  86.2236  91.9838  87.1034  88.53  85.7026  92.7969  93.3154  93.3688
```

(c) `rip_test_liver_segmentation.dat`

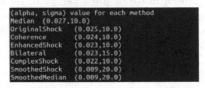

```latex
\documentclass{standalone}
\begin{document}
\begin{tabular}{c|c}
\hline
\bf Name & \bf $(\alpha,\sigma)$ \\
\hline
\hline
Median        & (0.027,10.0) \\
OriginalShock & (0.025,10.0) \\
Coherence     & (0.024,10.0) \\
EnhancedShock & (0.023,10.0) \\
Bilateral     & (0.023,15.0) \\
ComplexShock  & (0.022,10.0) \\
SmoothedShock & (0.009,20.0) \\
SmoothedMedian & (0.009,20.0) \\
\end{tabular}
\end{document}
```

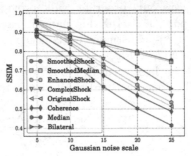

(d) Outputs for image denoising

Fig. 6. Input data files for the three tests of robustness presented in this article (a–c). Comments (lines starting by '#') have been removed in this figure, for a sake of clarity. In (d), the outputs are a table written in LaTeX summarizing the robustness test (left); a figure for a visual inspection of robustness and an output in the console (right).

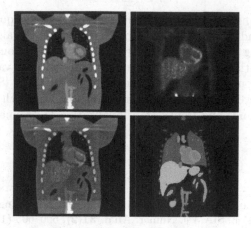

Fig. 7. Simulations of FDG-PET (FluoroDeoxyGlucose - Positron Emission Tomography) and CT (right and left respectively) by VIP, from [8].

6 Discussion

In this paper, we have introduced a novel approach to measure robustness of image processing algorithms. We have first proposed to model image uncertainty, which encompasses the classic additive Gaussian noise alteration. Second, we have refined the factors we calculate for a given algorithm. Beside the quality loss obtained by considering Lipschitz continuity over the scales of uncertainties, we also keep the scale where this worst decrease appears. This permits to study the weakness of a method, and for which kind of image data it may happen in a concrete application.

As future concern, we would like to compare our measure with other approaches, such as calculating area under the curve, or by summing the successive quality variations. For both image enhancement and segmentation, we have conducted our study with datasets of limited size, and we have to confirm our results with larger image collections. We also hope that the code freely downloadable at [24] will help researchers and engineers to address more easily this problem of robustness for image processing in their activity.

Furthermore, it would be interesting to study noises inherent to acquisition machines from a multi-scale point of view, as Rician noise in MRI (magnetic resonance imaging) for instance [5,9]. Drawing a relation between organ shape variability and robust image processing is another important question that is not studied in such a way in the literature. Our first measure of variability can be obviously applied to any other organ than the liver, and should be enhanced by further researches. More precisely, we could increase the number of parameters to represent complex organic shapes, but using more sophisticated models, such as [4] for instance. Robustness could be thus studied at a (slightly) greater dimension, to better understand the variation of image processing's outcomes.

Whatever the uncertainty studied, it is necessary to acquire a voluminous amount of data, and to annotate it in order to determine algorithms' robustness. For completing such a database, we could use simulation, as VIP (Virtual Imaging Platform) that consists in generating images, with various parameters related to acquisition machine and target organ's anatomy [8] (see Fig. 7). To do so, we would have to inject in this simulator data from the target modality (CT, MRI, ultrasound) and from organ localization (*e.g.* binary masks of liver volume).

References

1. Alvarez, L., Mazorra, L.: Signal and image restoration using shock filters and anisotropic diffusion. SIAM J. Numer. Anal. **31**(2), 590–605 (1994)
2. Bishop, C.: Pattern Recognition and Machine Learning. Springer, New York (2006)
3. Carlini, N., Wagner, D.: Towards evaluating the robustness of neural networks. In: IEEE Security and Privacy (2017)
4. Cartade, C., Mercat, C., Malgouyres, R., Samir, C.: Mesh parameterization with generalized discrete conformal maps. J. Math. Imaging Vis. **46**(1), 1–11 (2013)
5. Coupé, P., Manjón, J., Gedamu, E., Arnold, D., Robles, M., Collins, D.: Robust rician noise estimation for MR images. Med. Image Anal. **14**(4), 483–493 (2010)
6. Fawzi, A., Moosavi-Dezfooli, S.M., Frossard, P.: The robustness of deep networks: a geometrical perspective. IEEE Signal Process. Mag. **34**, 50–62 (2017)
7. Gilboa, G., Sochen, N.A., Zeevi, Y.Y.: Regularized shock filters and complex diffusion. In: Heyden, A., Sparr, G., Nielsen, M., Johansen, P. (eds.) ECCV 2002. LNCS, vol. 2350, pp. 399–413. Springer, Heidelberg (2002). https://doi.org/10.1007/3-540-47969-4_27
8. Glatard, T., et al.: A virtual imaging platform for multi-modality medical image simulation. IEEE Trans. Med. Imaging **32**(1), 110–118 (2013)
9. Gudbjartsson, H., Patz, S.: The rician distribution of noisy MRI data. Magn. Reson. Med. **34**(6), 910–914 (1995)
10. He, B., et al.: Fast automatic 3D liver segmentation based on a three-level AdaBoost-guided active shape model. Med. Phys. **43**(5), 2421–2434 (2016)
11. Heimann, T., et al.: Comparison and evaluation of methods for liver segmentation from CT datasets. IEEE Trans. Med. Imaging **28**(8), 1251–1265 (2009)
12. Huang, T., Yang, G., Tang, G.: A fast two-dimensional median filtering algorithm. IEEE Trans. Acoust. Speech Signal Process. **27**(1), 13–18 (1979)
13. 3D-IRCADb 01 (2018). http://www.ircad.fr/research/3d-ircadb-01/
14. Kass, M., Solomon, J.: Smoothed local histogram filters. ACM Trans. Graph. **29**(4), 100:1–100:10 (2010)
15. Lebre, M.-A., et al.: Medical image processing and numerical simulation for digital hepatic parenchymal blood flow. In: Tsaftaris, S.A., Gooya, A., Frangi, A.F., Prince, J.L. (eds.) SASHIMI 2017. LNCS, vol. 10557, pp. 99–108. Springer, Cham (2017). https://doi.org/10.1007/978-3-319-68127-6_11
16. Lebrun, M., Colom, M., Buades, A., Morel, J.: Secrets of image denoising cuisine. Acta Numer. **21**, 475–576 (2012)
17. Limare, N.: Reproducible research, software quality, online interfaces and publishing for image processing. Ph.D. thesis, École normale supérieure de Cachan, France (2012)

18. Lu, D., Weng, Q.: A survey of image classification methods and techniques for improving classification performance. Int. J. Remote. Sens. **28**(5), 823–870 (2007)
19. Malmberg, F., Nordenskjöld, R., Strand, R., Kullberg, J.: Smartpaint: a tool for interactive segmentation of medical volume images. Comput. Methods Biomech. Biomed. Eng. Imaging Vis. **5**(1), 36–44 (2014)
20. Meer, P.: From a robust hierarchy to a hierarchy of robustness. In: Davis, L.S. (ed.) Foundations of Image Understanding. The Springer International Series in Engineering and Computer Science, vol. 628, pp. 323–347. Springer, Boston (2001). https://doi.org/10.1007/978-1-4615-1529-6_11
21. Meer, P.: Robust techniques for computer vision. In: Emerging Topics in Computer Vision, pp. 107–190. Prentice Hall (2004)
22. Menze, B., et al. (eds.): Medical Computer Vision: Algorithms for Big Data. LNCS, vol. 8848. Springer, Cham (2014). https://doi.org/10.1007/978-3-319-13972-2
23. Osher, S., Rudin, L.: Feature-oriented image enhancement using shock filters. SIAM J. Numer. Anal. **27**, 919–940 (1990)
24. Robust image processing (2019). https://github.com/antoinevacavant/robustimageprocessing
25. Thomas, R., McSharry, P.: Big Data Revolution: What Farmers, Doctors and Insurance Agents Teach Us About Discovering Big Data Patterns. Wiley, Hoboken (2015)
26. Toennies, K.D.: Guide to Medical Image Analysis. Springer, London (2012). https://doi.org/10.1007/978-1-4471-2751-2
27. Tomasi, C., Manduchi, R.: Bilateral filtering for gray and color images. In: IEEE International Conference on Computer Vision, Bombay, India (1998)
28. Vacavant, A.: A novel definition of robustness for image processing algorithms. In: Kerautret, B., Colom, M., Monasse, P. (eds.) RRPR 2016. LNCS, vol. 10214, pp. 75–87. Springer, Cham (2017). https://doi.org/10.1007/978-3-319-56414-2_6
29. Vacavant, A.: Robust image processing: Definition, algorithms and evaluation. Université Clermont Auvergne, France, Habilitation (2018)
30. Vacavant, A., Albouy-Kissi, A., Menguy, P., Solomon, J.: Fast smoothed shock filtering. In: IEEE International Conference on Pattern Recognition, Tsukuba, Japan (2012)
31. Wang, Z.: Mean squared error: love it or leave it? A new look at signal fidelity measures. IEEE Signal Process. Mag. **26**(1), 98–117 (2009)
32. Weickert, J.: Coherence-enhancing shock filters. In: Michaelis, B., Krell, G. (eds.) DAGM 2003. LNCS, vol. 2781, pp. 1–8. Springer, Heidelberg (2003). https://doi.org/10.1007/978-3-540-45243-0_1

ReScience C: A Journal for Reproducible Replications in Computational Science

Nicolas P. Rougier[1,2,3]([✉])(iD) and Konrad Hinsen[4,5]([✉])(iD)

[1] INRIA Bordeaux Sud-Ouest, Talence, France
Nicolas.Rougier@inria.fr
[2] Institut des Maladies Neurodégénératives, Université de Bordeaux,
CNRS UMR 5293, Bordeaux, France
[3] LaBRI, Université de Bordeaux, Bordeaux INP, CNRS UMR 5800, Talence, France
[4] Centre de Biophysique Moléculaire, CNRS UPR 4301, Orléans, France
Konrad.Hinsen@cnrs.fr
[5] Synchrotron SOLEIL, Division Expériences, Gif sur Yvette, France

Abstract. Independent replication is one of the most powerful methods to verify published scientific studies. In computational science, it requires the reimplementation of the methods described in the original article by a different team of researchers. Replication is often performed by scientists who wish to gain a better understanding of a published method, but its results are rarely made public. ReScience C is a peer-reviewed journal dedicated to the publication of high-quality computational replications that provide added value to the scientific community. To this end, ReScience C requires replications to be reproducible and implemented using Open Source languages and libraries. In this article, we provide an overview of ReScience C's goals and quality standards, outline the submission and reviewing processes, and summarize the experience of its first three years of operation, concluding with an outlook towards evolutions envisaged for the near future.

Keywords: Open Science · Computational science · Reproducibility

1 Introduction

The question of how to attain reliable outcomes from unreliable components pervades many aspects of life. Scientific research is no exception. Individual research contributions are prone to mistakes, and sometimes fraud, and therefore error detection and correction mechanisms are required to reach a higher level of reliability at the collective level. The two main methods for error detection are critical inspection, starting with peer review of article submissions but continuing well after publication, and independent replication of published work. But replication is more than a verification technique. For the researchers performing the replication, it yields a level of understanding and insight that is impossible to achieve by other means. This is in fact the main motivation for much replication work, verification being merely a side effect.

B. Kerautret et al. (Eds.): RRPR 2018, LNCS 11455, pp. 150–156, 2019.
https://doi.org/10.1007/978-3-030-23987-9_14

The power but also the limitations of replication as an approach to verification are best illustrated by the recent discussion of replication crises in various scientific domains [3,5,6,9], which are all based on the observation of frequent failures to replicate published scientific findings. However, a replication failure does not necessarily mean that the original study is flawed. First of all, it could well be the replication work that is at fault. But it is also possible that both the original and the replication work are of excellent quality and yet yield different conclusions, if some important factor has escaped everyone's attention and accidentally differs between the two studies (see [10,12] for a recent example that led to a seven-year search for the cause of the disagreement). In this situation, independent replication can become the starting point of completely new lines of research.

Replication is thus an important contribution to science, and its findings should be shared with the scientific community. Unfortunately, most journals do not accept replication studies for publication because originality is one of their selection criteria. For this reason, we launched ReScience in 2015 (now called ReScience C for reasons explained later) as a journal dedicated to replications of computational research. In this article, we outline its mode of operation and summarize our experience from the first few years. A more complete account, also containing more background references, has been published recently [11].

2   Terminology: Reproducible Replications

The replication crisis has given rise to an active debate in various domains of science, in which some terms, in particular "reproducible" and "replicable", are used with very different meanings. We therefore explain the definitions that we are using in this article and more generally in ReScience C. Our definitions are formulated in the specific context of computational science, and are not easily transferable to experimental science [4].

A computation is *reproducible* if the code and input data is available together with sufficient instructions for someone else to re-do or *reproduce* the computation. The only point in reproducing the computation is to verify its reproducibility, which in turn is evidence that the archived code and data is (1) complete and (2) indeed the code and data that was used in the original published study. A failed reproduction means that the description of the original code and data is incomplete or inaccurate. A frequent form of incompleteness is the lack of a detailed description of the computational environment, i.e. the infrastructure software (operating system, compiler, ...) or code dependencies (libraries, ...) that were used in the original work. Reproducible computations are the most detailed and accurate possible description of a computational method within the current state of the art of computational science.

A *replication* of computational work involves writing and then running new software, using only the description of a method published in a journal article, i.e. without using or consulting the software used by the original authors, which may or may not be available. Successful replication confirms that the method description is complete and accurate, and significantly reduces the probability of an error in either implementation. A replication failure can be caused by such errors or by an inexact or incomplete method description. It requires further investigation which, as explained above, can even lead to new directions of scientific inquiry.

A *reproducible replication* is a replication whose code and data has been archived and documented for reproducibility. It is especially useful in the still dominant situation that the target of the replication was not published reproducibly. In that case, the replication provides not only verification, but also the missing code and data.

3   ReScience C

The definition of a replication given above should be sufficient to show that performing replications is a useful activity for a researcher. Moreover, whether successful or not, a replication yields additional insight into the problem that are worth sharing with the scientific community. For example, minor omissions or inaccuracies are inevitable in the narratives that make up for most of a journal article, meaning that replication authors have to do some detective work whose results are of use to others.

Unfortunately, the vast majority of scientific journals would not consider such work for publication, with the possible exception of a failed replication of particularly important findings, because novelty is for them an important selection criterion. Moreover, the reviewing process of traditional scientific journals, designed in the 20th century for experimental and theoretical but not for computational work, cannot handle the technical challenges posed by a verification of reproducibility and successful replication. For these reasons we created the ReScience C journal (at the time called simply ReScience) in September 2015 as a state-of-the-art venue for the publication of reproducible replication studies in computational science.

The criteria that a submission must fulfill for acceptance by ReScience C are the following:

- It must aim at reproducing all or a significant part of the figures and tables in an already published scientific study.
- The text of the article must discuss which results were successfully replicated and which, if any, could not be replicated. It should also provide a description of problems that were encountered, e.g. additional assumptions that had to be made.
- The complete source code of the software used for the replication must be provided, and should have only Open Source software as dependencies in order to allow full inspection of the complete software stack.
- In order to ensure the independence of the replication, its authors should not include any authors of the original study, nor their close collaborators.

A newly submitted replication is assigned to a member of the editorial board, which at this time is composed of 12 scientists from different research domains. The handling editor recruits two reviewers from a pool of currently nearly 100 volunteers. The reviewing process consists of a dialog between the reviewers, the authors, and the handling editor whose goal is to improve the submission to the point that it can be accepted. In particular, the reviewers verify that they can reproduce the results from the supplied code and data, and judge if the replication claims made by the authors are valid subject to the criteria of their scientific domain. The entire reviewing process is openly conducted on the GitHub platform, meaning that contributions are open to read for anyone, and anyone with a GitHub account can participate by leaving a comment. Once the submission is deemed acceptable, it is added to the table of contents and to the ReScience archive, with links to the submission repository, the review, and a PDF version which permits the article to handled like a standard scientific paper in personal and institutional databases and bibliography management software. An additional copy is deposited on Zenodo [2], which, being an archiving platform, makes stronger promises about long-term preservation than GitHub, whose primary goal is to support dynamic development processes. An additional advantage is that Zenodo issues a DOI that serves as a persistent reference.

The outstanding feature of this reviewing process, even compared to other journals practicing open peer review, is the rapid interaction between reviewers and authors that does not require the constant intervention of the handling editor. This rapid exchange has turned out to be essential in the quick resolution of the technical issues that inevitably arise when dealing with software and data.

Another outstanding feature of ReScience C is its reliance on no other infrastructure than two digital platforms, GitHub and Zenodo, which are both free to use. Considering that editors and reviewers as well as authors are unpaid volunteers, this means that ReScience C has so far been able to operate without any budget at all, and thereby avoid being subjected to any political pressure. We note however that this may not always be true for the individual volunteers contributing to ReScience C because the open reviewing process provides no anonymity. It is therefore imaginable that authors or reviewers of a ReScience article pointing out a mistake in prior work by an influential scientist could be exposed to sanctions by that scientist in grant or tenure reviews.

4 Learning from the Past to Prepare the Future

After three years of operation, our original ideas for ReScience C have turned into concrete practical experience which has mostly confirmed our expectations. It has also shown a few weaknesses, most of which concern technical details, which we are currently addressing in an overhaul of the ReScience C publishing workflow. In the following we summarize this experience and the conclusions we have drawn from it, referring to the full account [11] for the details.

ReScience C has so far published 27 articles. Most submissions are from computational neuroscience, the other represented domains are neuroimaging, computational ecology, and computer graphics. No submission was ever rejected. All submitted replications were successful, but this is probably due to a selection bias: publishing a failed replication is equivalent to publicly accusing the authors of the target work of having made a mistake, which is a potential source of conflict. One idea we have put forward to alleviate this obstacle is pre-publication replication. In that scenario, researchers submit their original work to a new type of journal, for which we use the name CoScience to indicate that we imagine it as the successor of ReScience. The journal then invites other scientists to do a replication, and publishes the original work and the replication together as a single joint work by the original authors and the replication team.

Achieving reproducibility has been much more challenging than expected. It is the reviewers' task to verify reproducibility, but our experience has shown that this is not sufficient to ensure that someone else can reproduce the work as well. Reviewers typically work in the same field as the authors and are likely to have similar software installation on their computers, meaning that unlisted dependencies can easily go unnoticed. There are a few approaches that would improve reproducibility, but each has its downsides as well. IPOL [8] provides online execution via its Web site, which is extremely convenient for both reviewers and readers. However, it is feasible only because IPOL's narrow domain scope (signal processing) makes the restriction to a small number of computational environments (C/C++, Python, Matlab) acceptable. We could also impose higher technical reproducibility guarantees on authors, e.g. the submission of an archived environment in the form of a virtual machine or a container image, which would also open the door to online execution via services such as Binder [1]. Such a requirement might, however, also become an additional barrier discouraging researchers from publishing their replication work.

The open reviewing process has overall worked very well. The exchanges between reviewers and authors have been constructive and courteous without exception. The handling editor intervenes mainly at the beginning, by inviting reviewers, and at the end, by judging if the reviewers' feedback is satisfactory for publication. Occasionally, reviewers or authors ask the handling editor for help with specific, mostly technical, issues. Another common task for the handling editor is to gently nudge authors or reviewers towards completing their tasks within reasonable delays. It is rare for third parties to intervene, but in one case a reviewer suggested asking the author of the target study for the permission to re-use some data, which he did by commenting directly on the GitHub platform.

An unexpected and so far unresolved consequence of the open reviewing process is the impossibility to handle replications that process confidential data. In some fields of science, confidentiality is inevitable, be it for ethical reasons (e.g. in medical research) or for commercial ones (e.g. data on stock market transactions not freely available). This is an issue of wider concern for the Open Science community, and we hope that satisfactory solutions will emerge in the near future.

The use of the GitHub platform has turned out to be a good choice overall. Since a ReScience C submission combines a narrative and source code, with the code taking center stage during the reviewing process, a platform designed for collaborative software development and code reviewing is a better match than the traditional manuscript management platforms used by scientific journals, which have no provision at all for reviewing code. We are, however, currently revising several technical details. Submissions currently take the form of a pull request to the ReScience repository, which is counter intuitive for an article submission. More importantly, the final steps of publishing in our current workflow are laborious and not automated, causing too much hassle mainly for the handling editor. In the future workflow, articles are submitted as individual repositories of which ReScience retains a fork upon acceptance.

Finally, an evolution that has motivated the name change from ReScience to ReScience C is the imminent launch of ReScience X, a new journal dedicated to replications of experimental research, under the auspices of Etienne Roesch and Nicolas Rougier. We hope that it will be able to profit from the experience gained with ReScience C, although the challenges it will face are of a quite different nature. ReScience C will continue to focus on improving computational research, joining forces with the wider Reproducible Research community wherever possible. For example, we envisage proposing the publication of dedicated issues to reproducibility-related workshops such as the Reproducible Research on Pattern Recognition workshop [7] (part of the International Conference on Pattern Recognition) or the Enabling Reproducibility in Machine Learning workshop (part of the International Conference on Machine Learning).

References

1. Binder. https://mybinder.org/
2. Zenodo. http://www.zenodo.org/
3. Baker, M.: 1,500 scientists lift the lid on reproducibility. Nature **533**(7604), 452–454 (2016). https://doi.org/10.1038/533452a
4. Hinsen, K.: Scientific software is different from lab equipment, May 2018. http://blog.khinsen.net/posts/2018/05/07/scientific-software-is-different-from-lab-equipment/
5. Ioannidis, J.P.A.: Why most published research findings are false. Plos Med **2**(8), e124 (2005). https://doi.org/10.1371/journal.pmed.0020124
6. Iqbal, S.A., Wallach, J.D., Khoury, M.J., Schully, S.D., Ioannidis, J.P.A.: Reproducible research practices and transparency across the biomedical literature. PLOS Biol. **14**(1), e1002333 (2016). https://doi.org/10.1371/journal.pbio.1002333
7. Kerautret, B., Colom, M., Monasse, P. (eds.): RRPR 2016. LNCS, vol. 10214. Springer, Cham (2017). https://doi.org/10.1007/978-3-319-56414-2
8. Limare, N., Oudre, L., Getreuer, P.: IPOL: reviewed publication and public testing of research software. In: 2012 IEEE 8th International Conference on E-Science, pp. 1–8. IEEE, Chicago, October 2012. https://doi.org/10.1109/eScience.2012.6404449
9. Munafò, M.R., et al.: A manifesto for reproducible science. Nat. Hum. Behav. **1**(1), 0021 (2017). https://doi.org/10.1038/s41562-016-0021
10. Palmer, J.C., et al.: Comment on "The putative liquid-liquid transition is a liquid-solid transition in atomistic models of water" [I and II: J. Chem. Phys. **135**, 134503 (2011); J. Chem. Phys. **138**, 214504 (2013)]. J. Chem. Phys. **148**(13), 137101 (2018). https://doi.org/10.1063/1.5029463

11. Rougier, N.P., et al.: Sustainable computational science: the ReScience initiative. PeerJ Comput. Sci. **3**, e142 (2017). https://doi.org/10.7717/peerj-cs.142
12. Smart, A.G.: The war over supercooled water. Phys. Today (2018). https://doi.org/10.1063/PT.6.1.20180822a

Author Index

Printed in the United States
By Bookmasters